THE BATTLE OF JUTLAND

THE BATTLE OF JUTLAND

❖

Geoffrey Bennett

WORDSWORTH EDITIONS

First published in the United Kingdom in 1964
B. T. Batsford Limited

Second impression published in 1972
by David & Charles (Publishers) Limited

This edition published 1999
by Wordsworth Editions Limited
Cumberland House, Crib Street, Ware,
Hertfordshire SG12 9ET

ISBN 1 84022 204 2

Printed and bound in Great Britain
by Mackays of Chatham plc, Chatham, Kent.

PREFACE TO THE FIRST EDITION

Since a reviewer of a previous book of mine, *Coronel and the Falklands*, observed 'it is doubtful if another book on the subject is justified', a word to disarm the same criticism of *The Battle of Jutland* – to the Germans, Skagerrak – will not come amiss. Although not decisive, as were Nelson's battles, the only major naval action of the First World War has a unique claim to attention. In 1805, 27 British ships-of-the-line with a maximum burden of 2,250 tons annihilated 33 ships from France and Spain in the last fleet action fought in open water before sail gave way to steam. A century later Togo, with 4 battleships as large as 16,000 tons and 8 armoured cruisers, destroyed the same number of Russian vessels in the principal naval engagement in the 100 years before the completion of the *Dreadnought*. In contrast, no fewer than 64 capital ships, one displacing 28,500 tons, met in combat at Jutland on 31st May 1916. In short, this was the biggest battle at sea since Henry VIII armed his ships with 'great guns'. It was also the last before nations could no longer afford battleships in such numbers, before aircraft deprived them of their paramount power, and before guided missiles and nuclear weapons transformed the pattern of maritime warfare. In 1864 it was clear that the world would never again see a fleet such as that of which the *Victory* remains a lasting memorial. Today it is certain that none will see again the massive dreadnoughts with which Jellicoe and Beatty fought Scheer and Hipper nearly 50 years ago.

There is, however, a more important justification for this book. The present writer is the first, with the distinguished exception of the late Sir Julian Corbett (*Naval Operations*, Vol. III – more than forty years ago), to produce an acount of the battle with the advantage of access to the papers of the late Vice-Admiral J. E. T. Harper. These relate to the suppression of the original *Harper Record* prepared in 1919, as well as to the equally suppressed secret *Naval Staff Appreciation of Jutland* (1923), a checkered story sketched in Appendix III – though it should not be inferred that I have accepted all the strictures on the conduct of the battle which the latter contains.

My first chapter summarizes the circumstances in which Germany elected to challenge British sea power in August 1914; my second covers operations in the North Sea up to 31st May 1916. Both are needed for a proper understanding of Jutland,

and my account is enriched by the personal recollections of those who fought under Jellicoe and Scheer, of which one must have pride of place here:

The Jutland battle was a great thing to have been in; it was very different from what I expected. We in the Collingwood *saw a good deal more than some of the other ships and we fired more than they did. We were not hit at all, which was very lucky, though we were straddled several times. One shell dropped over the forecastle, missing us by inches. I was in the fore turret, second-in-command. During some part of it I was sitting on top when they straddled us. I didn't remain up very long after that! We had no breakdowns of any sort. Everything worked very well; as for the men, they were quite marvellous, just as cheery as usual and worked like demons. The worst part of it was the night afterwards. we ceased firing at 9 p.m. and went to night defence until 2 a.m. when we closed up in the turrets again. We were sick at not seeing the enemy again that morning.*

This account by the future King George VI, then Sub-Lieutenant Prince Albert, recalls the words of the Spanish Admiral Langara at Gibralta in 1780 when he found the embryo King William IV serving as a midshipman in the *Prince George* in which he was present at the Battle of Cape St Vincent: 'Well does Great Britain merit the Empire of the Sea when the humblest stations in her navy are supported by Princes of the Blood.'

My final chapter attempts an assessment of the battle and 'reasons why'. Though I have done my best to be fair to both sides, this cannot be wholly objective – so much is not to be expected of a British writer. It has, however, one advantage over the work of the majority of previous Jutland historians; I was born too late to suffer the bias which blinded them in favour of either Jellicoe or Beatty. This is not to claim that I have written the definitive account of a battle which both so ably fought, as did their German opponents. More than 100 years elapsed before an Admiralty Commission issued such a version of Trafalgar; as long may elapse before the last word is said about Jutland.

For reasons of space I have abbreviated quotations from documents and other sources without disfiguring them with ellipses. I have not, of course, distorted their sense.

GEOFFREY BENNETT
London 1964

PREFACE TO THIS EDITION

'Who won the battle of Jutland?'

I still recall posing that apparently simple question to the naval history instructor during my national service in the Royal Navy.

Of course his answer was not nearly so uncomplicated; though Britain lost the most ships, Jellicoe did not, as Churchill had feared he could, lose the war in an afternoon. The failure of the German High Seas Fleet to put to sea again and its final disintegration into mutiny were enough to play a vital part in British victory.

The best short answer must be that concept, one that tyro-students of military affairs can have difficulty in comprehending, of a tactical defeat but a strategic victory.

When I was able to read my father's book some years later I had a much clearer understanding of it all.

Perhaps his greatest discovery was the Dewar brother's *Naval Staff Appreciation* of which all copies were supposed to have been destroyed. This was intriguing not because it offered any dramatic new insights (the brothers later published other writings on the battle covering similar ground) but showing that someone – he showed me the copy but never even told me who had lent it to him – was not prepared to tolerate the complete obliteration of something of significant historical interest if not great importance.

As my father says, he had the advantage of having been a serving officer during the war but no vested interest in what almost may be termed the second battle of Jutland – the subsequent feud between supporters of Jellicoe and Beatty. In addition, as his speciality was signals, he was particularly well-qualified to deal with this important aspect.

In Germany, where apparently literature on the subject is surpassingly limited, the book appeared in the 1970s as *Die Skagerrak Schlacht* (in Germany it is known as the Battle of Skagerrak). It was translated by R. K. Lochner and attracted some interest. If public lending rights payments are any guide, it still does. So, a welcome further English publication will give a new generation of naval history enthusiasts a chance to study a clear and comprehensive account of this seminal event.

RODNEY M. BENNETT
Richmond, London 1998

ACKNOWLEDGEMENTS

The author wishes to thank the following:

Her Majesty the Queen for gracious permission to quote from the letters and diaries of King George V and King George VI.

The Admiralty, especially the Naval Secretary, Rear-Admiral J. O. C. Hayes, and the Librarian, Lieutenant-Commander P. K. Kemp, for their help.

The Council of the Royal United Service Institution for access to the papers appertaining to the *Harper Record* left in their trust by the late Vice-Admiral J. E. T. Harper.

The late Admiral Sir William Tennant for the loan of the series of lectures on Jutland which he delivered to the Royal Naval Staff College.

The Earls Jellicoe and Beatty for access to the papers of Admirals of the Fleet Lord Jellicoe and Lord Beatty, for permission to quote from them, and for other help.

The late Admiral Sir Frederic Dreyer for many personal recollections of Admiral Jellicoe and Jutland whilst assisting with his autobiography, *The Sea Heritage*.

Professor Arthur Marder amd Mrs John Marsden-Smedley for letters written by the late Rear-Admiral the Hon. Barry Bingham.

Miss Mary Rundle for the recollections of Jutland written by her father the late Engineer Rear-Admiral Mark Rundle, and for her own memories of Admiral Beatty.

Commander W. D. M. Staveley for the loan of Admiral Sir Doveton Sturdee's papers.

My father, Rear-Admiral M. G. Bennett; Brigadier J. Stephenson, Director of the Royal United Service Institution, and his library staff; all for help and advice.

The Imperial War Museum Photographic Library staff for assistance in tracing illustrations.

The Controller, H. M. Stationery Office, for permission to quote from *Naval Operations* (Vol. III) by Julian Corbett, and from other documents which are Crown Copyright.

Authors and publishers of other works from which I have quoted, in particular: Winston S. Churchill, and Odhams Books Ltd. (*The World Crisis, 1911-1918*); William Heinemann Ltd. (*From Snotty to Sub* by 'Heandi'); 'Bartimeus' and Hodder and Stoughton, Ltd. (*The Navy Eternal*); Rear-Admiral W. S. Chalmers and Hodder and Stoughton Ltd. (*The Life and Letters of David Beatty*); Cassell & Co. Ltd. (*Germany's High Seas Fleet in the*

World War by Admiral Scheer); Commander Sir Stephen King-Hall and Messrs Methuen & Co. Ltd. (*A Naval Lieutenant* by 'Etienne'); the Hutchinson Group (*The Fighting at Jutland* edited by H. W. Fawcett and G. W. W. Hooper, and *Kiel and Jutland* by Commander von Hase); the Trustees of Admiral Sir Frederic Dreyer (*The Sea Heritage*); Mr Desmond Young and Cassell & Co. Ltd. (*Rutland of Jutland*).

Miss Adrienne Edye for typing my manuscript; Miss Mary Rundle for compiling the Index; Mr Arthur banks for the diagrams; and Lieutenant-Commander A. B. Sainsbury for checking the proofs.

Far from least, my wife for her unfailing encouragement.

CONTENTS

THE ILLUSTRATIONS

The Author and Publishers wish to thank the following for permission to reproduce the illustrations:

Captain Garnons-Williams for fig. 28

Fine Arts Publishing Company for fig. 16

Imperial War Museum for figs. 1, 2, 6–15, 17, 18, 20–23, 26, 27 and 29

Suddeutscher Verlag, Munich for figs. 4 and 24

Verlag Ullstein, Berlin for figs. 3, 5, 19 and 25

DIAGRAMS

The title-page drawing is the crest of the Royal Navy's Signal School before it was commissioned as H.M.S. *Mercury*. The flags are those of Admiral Jellicoe's deployment signal at Jutland, 'Equal Speed Charlie London' (*vide* Chapter 4). For heraldic reasons H.M.S. *Mercury*'s shield bears a caduceus but Jellicoe's signal is still flown from the School's masthead on special occasions.

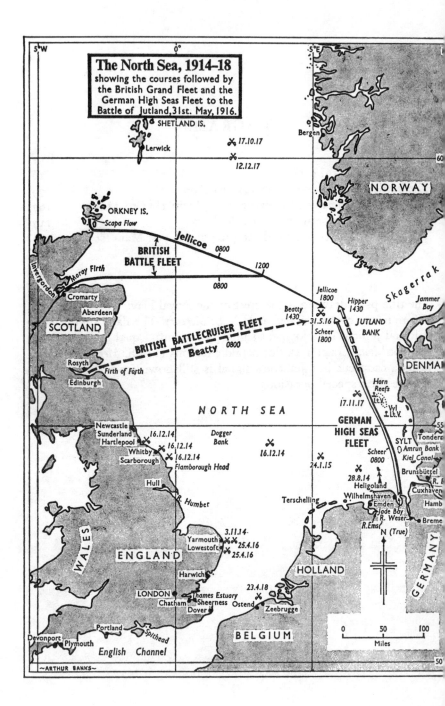

The North Sea, 1914–18
showing the courses followed by the British Grand Fleet and the German High Seas Fleet to the Battle of Jutland, 31st. May, 1916.

I

Genesis

'Our future lies on the water; the trident must be in our hands.'

Kaiser Wilhelm II in 1892

'The only thing in the world that England has to fear is Germany.'

Admiral Sir John Fisher in 1907

OF ALL the reasons advanced for the First World War one is not disputed, Germany's decision to challenge the sea power upon which Britain counted for security from invasion and to protect her Empire and her trade. In the 50 years following Trafalgar, which climaxed the Royal Navy's three-century struggle for maritime supremacy, the wooden-hulled ship-of-the-line remained the principal type of war vessel. In the fleets which Dundas took to the Crimea and Napier to the Baltic in 1854 there was only one significant difference from that with which Nelson and Collingwood triumphed over Villeneuve: some of their line-of-battle ships were fitted with steam as an auxiliary to sail; otherwise they were little more than larger and more heavily armed versions of the *Henry Grace à Dieu* of 1514. But those few steam-driven vessels heralded a revolution in warship design; in the next 45 years sail joined oars in the limbo of obsolete methods of propulsion; by the end of the nineteenth century the whole of the Royal Navy was driven by steam. This transformation was accompanied by two other innovations. 'Wooden walls' had sufficed to withstand the cast-iron balls of Nelson's smooth-bored cannon; explosive-filled shell from rifled guns compelled the fitting of armour to steel hulls. And the progress of gun manufacture allowed such an increase in size that the few which could be carried had to be mounted in revolving turrets, which meant the end of the three-decker with its multi-gunned broadsides. In 1805 the largest of the 'far-distant, storm-beaten ships upon which the Grand Army never looked' (*Mahan*) carried 120 guns, none bigger than a 32-pounder (carronades excepted), on a displacement of about 4,200 tons. By 1900, battleships displaced 13,000 tons, mounted four 12-inch plus twelve 6-inch guns and could steam at 18 knots.

Notwithstanding these developments Britain maintained her supremacy. Gladstone might try to reduce the Naval Estimates but public apprehension at the large fleet maintained by France whose ports were only a few hours steaming away, and by Russia who had designs on India and the Far East, was too strong. Successive scares, particularly that of 1885, compelled increases in the strength and readiness of the British Fleet. A navy capable of dealing with the fleets of any likely combination of Powers—Castlereagh's Two Power standard—was the only yardstick acceptable to a public which looked to its moat: in 1900 the Royal Navy counted more than 40 battleships against France's 26 and Russia's 12. Only Italy and the United States had as many as ten; Japan's six were more important because they required a comparable British force in the Far East. The remaining navies of the world were of no consequence, but percipient naval critics were already foretelling the meteoric growth of Germany's six battleships into a fleet second only to Britain's within so short a time as the next decade.

Behind this spectacular development was the unification of Germany (1867) and her rapid growth into a world Power. Napoleon III found a pretext for a tragic attempt to strangle Bismarck's brainchild four years after it was born. Six weeks of war ended the Second Empire; in as many months Paris capitulated, and France was compelled to cede Alsace and Lorraine and to allow King Wilhelm of Prussia to be crowned German Emperor at Versailles in 1871. The Iron Chancellor's ambitions were satisfied; in alliance with Austria and Italy, he aimed to preserve peace by isolating France, so that she was 'without friends and without allies', and by conciliating Russia. Germany's strength rested on her victorious army; with only five ironclads to Britain's 50 she could never aspire to command the sea. Nor was this necessary when the growth of German industry and commerce impelled Bismarck to found a modest colonial empire; by tactful diplomacy he avoided conflict with British interests.

Unfortunately Wilhelm I was succeeded in 1888 by a brash 29-year-old grandson whose actions were both reckless and impulsive, and whose considerable abilities were bedevilled by too arrogant a belief in his autocratic role. He could not stand aside whilst other European Powers grabbed Africa for themselves; he must have 'a place in the sun'. His first obstacle to an aggressive foreign policy, the ageing Bismarck's unchallenged authority, was soon removed: with scant courtesy, the wise old pilot was dropped in 1890. And Wilhelm was in no way perturbed when this drove France to negotiate with Russia, whereby in 1894 the Triple Alliance was opposed by a Dual Alliance which gave Germany a formidable enemy on each flank. The British Empire was an obstacle of a different order. The German Army could exert little influence on a people whose island heart was so well protected by a powerful fleet; nor was it of much value as an instrument of policy overseas so long as that fleet remained supreme. But the *Reichstag* was as reactionary as the federal *Diet* had been; it obstinately refused to vote funds for more than a small coast-defence force.

The Kaiser had, however, already found the man to realize his dream, Alfred von Tirpitz. Exceptionally able and energetic, he was a specialist in the two new weapons which the second half of the nineteenth century added to naval armouries, the torpedo and the mine, before he became a rear-admiral and held the post of Chief of Staff to the German Navy's High Command. Under his guidance realistic tactical exercises replaced formal manœuvres, every encouragement being given to subordinate commanders to act on their own initiative whenever they judged that they could further their commander-in-chief's intentions better in this way than by rigid compliance with his orders. Remembering how his own ship had been confined to Schillig Roads by the close blockade maintained by a much superior enemy fleet during the Franco-Prussian War, Tirpitz so fervently believed that Germany must build a High Seas Fleet if she was to maintain her growing power, that in 1897 the Kaiser appointed him Secretary of the Navy at the age of 48. And within a year he persuaded the *Reichstag* to authorize the construction of a fleet of 17 battleships to be completed in five years.

Despite Germany's nascent hostility, revealed by the Kruger telegram of 1896 and her curt rejection of conciliatory overtures in 1898 and 1899, Britain did not believe this Navy Law to be a serious threat. Such complacency was short-lived; whilst the Kaiser openly encouraged the Boers, Tirpitz used the seizure of German merchant vessels off the African coast to inflame the *Reichstag* into authorizing a fleet, headed by 34 battleships (later increased to 41 plus 20 heavy cruisers) which were to be completed by 1917. The preamble to his new Navy Law made their purpose plain: 'Germany must have a battle fleet so strong that, even for the strongest sea power, war against it would invite such dangers as to imperil its position in the world.' This challenge could not be ignored: Lord Salisbury's Cabinet responded by abandoning the policy of 'splendid isolation' conceived by Canning nearly a hundred years before, and firmly established by Palmerston with the impetus of Cobden and Bright after the Crimean War. To curtail Russia's ambitions in the East an alliance was forged with Japan in 1902-4. Salisbury's successor took a more momentous step: to avert the recurring danger of serious differences with France, Balfour made overtures to Paris. The resulting *Entente Cordiale*, whereby the Dual Alliance became a Triple Entente, was cemented at Algeciras in 1906, when an International Conference met to resolve the crisis provoked by the Kaiser's lack of tact in visiting Tangier when France was involved in a dispute with Morocco.

Whilst the Northcliffe Press, from *The Times* down to *The Boy's Friend*, and men like Erskine Childers in *The Riddle of the Sands*, alerted the British public to the German menace, the Government began to prepare for a future clash. Balfour's inspired creation of a Committee of Imperial Defence and the provision of a General Staff at the War Office were two much needed measures. Another was a decision to construct a naval base at Rosyth because Portsmouth and Devonport were too far away to support a fleet whose battleground would be the North Sea. But the naval consequences of the *Entente* were more important. For nearly a century the British Navy had maintained the *Pax Britannica* as effectively as the United States' possession of nuclear weapons and the North Atlantic Treaty Organization have prevented a major conflict since the end of the Second World War. Nonetheless, by the turn of the century 'though numerically a very imposing force, it was in certain respects a drowsy, inefficient, motheaten organism' (*Marder*). It had many splendid seamen willing to die for their country but few men of vision who looked to the future rather than the past. Without the stimulus of a major naval war its senior officers had failed to grapple with the changes required by rapid technological progress; they were content to live on Nelson's credit. War plans did not exist. Fighting efficiency and tactics had been neglected. Fleet exercises 'took the form of quadrille-like movements carried out in accordance with geometrical diagrams which entirely ignored all questions of gun and torpedo fire' (*Vice-Admiral K. G. B. Dewar*). 'Gunnery was merely a necessary evil; polo and pony racing were more important than gun drill' (*Admiral of the Fleet Sir Reginald Tyrwhitt*). When those who argued that masts and yards must be retained for training ships' companies were finally vanquished, some officers realized the Navy's short-comings. But Britain had to wait for one of the most remarkable men in all her history for the sweeping changes needed to restore her Fleet to an effective fighting machine.

'Jacky' Fisher was eight years older than Tirpitz. Joining the Royal Navy at the age of 13 'penniless, friendless and forlorn' (*his own phrase*), he became a captain at 33, commanding the *Inflexible* at the bombard-ment of Alexandria in 1882. He returned to be Director of Naval Ordnance, Admiral Superintendent of Portsmouth Dockyard, and Third Sea Lord, three appointments which gave him first-hand experience of the administrative apathy which was largely responsible for the marked inefficiency that characterized much of the Victorian Navy. Attaining flag rank in 1890, Fisher went back to sea in 1897 to command the North American and West Indies Station, and from there to be Commander-in-Chief Mediterranean, where he swept away much of the dust and cobwebs of antiquated thought and practice. Amongst his innovations were realistic fleet exercises, and an increase in gun range from a point-blank 2,000 yards to 6,000 to counter the danger of torpedo fire. As Admiral Sir John Fisher he returned to the Admiralty to be Second Sea Lord and to introduce the 'Selborne Scheme' which modernized the training of naval officers. In 1903 he became Commander-in-Chief Portsmouth when he served on the Esher Committee which reformed the War Office. One year more and this 'veritable volcano', with the perception of genius, became First Sea Lord; caring not that he 'left many foes foaming in his wake, [he] hoisted the storm signal and beat all hands to quarters' (*Churchill*).

Fisher presented his plans to the First Lord on his first day at the Admiralty. The French battle fleet was divided between the Channel, Atlantic and Mediterranean, the Russian between the Baltic, Black Sea and Pacific. So long as these were Britain's only rivals she could station half her battle fleet in the Mediterranean and a battle squadron in the Far East, and still have a sufficient force in Home Waters. Not so when 'the new German Navy is able to concentrate almost the whole of its fleet including all its battleships at its home ports', chiefly Kiel and

Wilhelmshaven, from where it could quickly emerge into the North Sea and threaten Britain's east coast. The Anglo-Japanese alliance and the destruction of the Russian Fleet in 1905 allowed Britain's battle-ships to be withdrawn from the Far East. The *Entente* was followed by an agreement that France would base her fleet on Toulon and accept responsibility for dealing with the Austrian Fleet, so that Britain could transfer most of her battleships to more northern waters. Whilst Sir Edward Grey, the Foreign Secretary, stated that this disposition was not 'based upon an engagement to co-operate in war', Churchill argued that 'the moral claims which France could make upon Great Britain if attacked by Germany were enormously extended'.

Fisher also disclosed that the Admiralty's distribution of ships abroad dated 'from a period when the electric telegraph did not exist and when wind was the motive power'. Third-class cruisers and sloops, however adequate for Palmerston's 'gunboat diplomacy', would be useless in war. In the steam age a few modern cruisers should be stationed at a number of strategic points from which in peace they could be quickly summoned anywhere by telegraph, and in war serve to protect the trade routes against marauding German cruisers. The wholesale scrapping of ships which could 'neither fight nor run away', that followed this redeployment, saved the men needed for another measure that increased Britain's readiness. Ships in full commission in peace became the First Fleet. Those lying in their home ports, which could be quickly manned by officers and men under training, were given nucleus crews so that they could be commissioned at short notice; these formed the Second Fleet which would reinforce the First whose task would be to oppose the High Seas Fleet. The older ships, which depended on mobilization for their crews, carried no more than small care and maintenance parties: this Third Fleet was for trade protection.

Fisher's plans included an epoch-making concept. Battleships completed before 1905 were armed with four 12-inch and twelve 6-inch guns. At near point-blank range this combination was an effective compromise between the devastating effect of the faster rate of fire of the smaller calibre weapons upon an enemy's unarmoured super-structure, and the heavier shell of the larger ones which were needed to pierce an armoured hull. But when the torpedo threat compelled an increase in range the scales tipped in favour of the heavier shell; the armament of the 'King Edward VII' class, completed 1905–6, was augmented by four 9·2-inch guns at the expense of two 6-inch, whilst the subsequent 'Lord Nelsons' were armed with ten 9·2-inch in addition to the customary four 12-inch, but no 6-inch. Meantime, the difficulty of distinguishing between the splashes from guns of different calibres at longer ranges, and so of controlling the fire of a mixed armament, had been appreciated. Fisher's solution was to arm battleships with guns of a single calibre. He also realized the tactical advantages of superior speed. From these desiderata the Admiralty evolved a battleship armed with ten 12-inch guns on a displacement of 17,900 tons and driven by turbines at 21 knots. The British Navy was not alone in conceiving an all big-gun battleship, but Fisher understood that such a radical change must render previous battleships obsolescent; if Britain was to maintain her superiority he must take special measures to ensure that H.M.S. *Dreadnought* was built so quickly and in such secrecy that Tirpitz would not know, before she was completed in 1906, that the German battle fleet would have to be designed anew. Britain was thus able to commission three more dreadnoughts of the 'Bellerophon' class before Germany's first two 'Westfalens', armed with 11-inch guns. Fisher also turned his attention to the armoured cruiser, a hybrid type for both scouting duties and as a fast wing to the battle line. To follow the 'Minotaur' class of 14,600 tons carrying a mixed armament of 9·2-inch and 7·5-inch guns at 23 knots, he ordered battlecruisers of 17,250 tons with eight 12-inch guns and a speed of 25 knots. The first three, the 'Invincible' class, were completed in 1908, whereas Germany's *Blücher* was not finished until 1909, with 8.2-inch guns, because Fisher had let it be supposed that the *Invincible* was to be so armed. When the 11-inch gunned *Von der Tann* was completed a year later, Britain had ten dreadnoughts in commission against Germany's six.

Though this margin compared unfavourably with the 53 pre-dread-noughts that Britain had opposed to Germany's 20 in 1905, it was not to be of much importance for all that Fisher was severely criticized for it by his bitter enemy, Lord Charles Beresford. The need to build larger battleships had posed Tirpitz another problem: Germany's harbours and the Kiel Canal had to be deepened and widened. Until this work was completed Germany could not hazard a naval war; and in the intervening four years much could happen to change the balance of dreadnought strength—and nearly did. Campbell-Bannerman's Administration had approved Lord Cawdor's programme of four capital ships a year; in 1908 Asquith's Cabinet, bent on expensive social reforms, was sufficiently convinced by one of the Kaiser's periodical assurances that his fleet was no challenge to Britain, to cut this to two, although in the same year the *Reichstag* authorized four. Fortunately Austria chose this moment to annex Bosnia and Herzegovina, which alarmed the British public into raising the cry, 'We want eight; we won't wait'. 'Till this moment the *Flottenpolitik* had been an anxiety; henceforth it was a nightmare' (*Gooch*). Asquith was compelled to give way. The Dominions, too, were roused: Australia and New Zealand offered to bear the cost of two battlecruisers whilst Malaya contributed a battleship. The impetus was thus maintained at five dreadnoughts a year, so that by the spring of 1912 the British Fleet included 17 dreadnoughts against Germany's 11. More important, although by July 1914 the fleet which Fisher had created comprised 29 dreadnoughts, the latest being armed with 13·5-inch guns, against which Germany opposed as many as 20 (albeit with no guns larger than 12-inch), 18 more were building in Britain, including 12 with 15-inch guns, whereas only seven were under construction in Germany of which only two had 15-inch guns.

By the time he retired in 1910 at the age of 69, Fisher had transformed Britain's antiquated Victorian navy into a twentieth-century fleet fit to meet its first serious challenge in a hundred years. But there was not enough time before 'Armageddon' (*his own word*) for his officer-training reforms to permeate the more senior ranks so that 'we had more captains of ships than captains of war' (*Churchill*). He foresaw the need for a Naval Staff at the Admiralty before he became First Sea Lord but took no steps to establish one in parallel with his recommendations for the War Office. His maxim, 'speed is armour', was to be proved fallacious. And he would not spend money on improving naval bases and docks so that Rosyth was still under construction in 1914.

As early as 1906 the German Ambassador in London, Count Metternich, began to warn his country that 'the real cause of the political tension is not commercial rivalry but the growing importance of our Navy'; but the Kaiser preferred the insidious reports of his Service Attachés that there was little to fear from Britain. Grey might say: 'Our Navy is to us what [the German] Army is to them. No superiority of the British Navy could ever put us in a position to affect the independence or integrity of Germany, because our Army is not maintained on a scale which, unaided, could do anything on German territory. *But if the German Navy were superior to ours, our independence, our very existence would be at stake.'* Yet Wilhelm II told Bülow 'that the alleged English agitation about our new [naval building] programme was simply bluff for reasons of English domestic policy. Such is the opinion of Tirpitz, and His Majesty is in entire agreement.' All Whitehall's overtures to Berlin aimed at alleviating naval rivalry were to no avail; the Kaiser dismissed them as 'groundless impertinence'. The Hague discussions in 1907 were torpedoed by Fisher's jingoistic utterances—including a suggestion that the best solution would be to 'Copenhagen the German Fleet *à la* Nelson' ('Fisher, you must be mad', commented King Edward VII). Others were spurned by Tirpitz who was angered by Churchill's reference to his *'Luxusflotte'*—'The British Navy is to us a necessity, whilst the German Navy is more in the nature of a luxury' (*Luxus* is more offensive than its English equivalent)—or wrecked by one of the Kaiser's disastrous interventions. The worst of these occurred in 1911 after France occupied Fez, when Germany sent the gunboat *Panther* to support her alleged, but *de facto* non-existent, interests in Agadir. In the crisis which this provoked Berlin ignored Grey's support for France until Lloyd-George spoke: 'If the situation were forced upon us in which peace could only be preserved by the surrender of the great and beneficent position Britain has won by centuries of heroism and achievement, by allowing Britain to be treated, where her interests were vitally affected, as if she were of no account in the Cabinet of Nations, then I say emphatically that peace at that price would be a humiliation intolerable for a great country like ours to endure.' When Germany climbed down Tirpitz accepted the rebuff with the philosophic comment: 'It was a question of keeping our nerves, continuing to arm on a grand scale and waiting without anxiety until our sea power was established.'

In London the crisis served an important purpose. Soon after the *Entente Cordiale* was established the ubiquitous Colonel Repington of *The Times* had taken it upon himself to arrange informal conversations between the British and French military staffs—'the thin edge of the insidious wedge of our taking part in a Continental war as apart from coastal military expeditions in concert with the Navy' (*Fisher*). These made such progress that the Cabinet recognized them; by 1911 the War Office had completed plans to send a British Expeditionary Force to fight by the side of the French Army in Flanders. But when these were expounded to the Cabinet by the Chief of the Imperial General Staff, Fisher's successor, Admiral of the Fleet Sir Arthur Wilson, declined to reveal the Admiralty's plans on the grounds that they were his sole responsibility. Pressed by the Prime Minister, he disclosed plans which 'savoured of having been "cooked up in the dinner hour"' (*Hankey*); in particular he had made no preparations to protect or support an Expeditionary Force, because he shared Fisher's view that the Army should be used as 'a projectile to be fired by the Navy: the Navy embarks it and lands it where it can do most mischief, instead of ineffectually opposing the vast Continental armies'. The Secretary of State for War, Lord Haldane, threatened resignation unless the Admiralty agreed to work in harmony with the War Office and introduce a Naval Staff. To achieve this Churchill was appointed First Lord, whilst 'Tug' Wilson, who for all his distinction had never used a staff and refused to have one at the Admiralty, was replaced by Admiral Sir Francis Bridgeman, who was followed in 1913 by Prince Louis of Battenberg. Thus, though Fisher's redeployment of the British Fleet laid the firmest of foundations for its use in war, the plans with which it began hostilities were not conceived until Churchill, Bridgeman and Battenberg headed the Admiralty.

By the summer of 1914 most people in Britain and Germany had come to regard war as inevitable, yet few realized its imminence. All Germany's dreadnoughts, 14 battleships and six battlecruisers, with the single exception of the battlecruiser *Goeben* in the Mediterranean, were divided between Kiel and Wilhelmshaven, the latter providing a North Sea base well protected by the heavily defended island of Heligoland, which Britain had 'won by the sword and given up by the pen' (*Fisher*). On 15th July, by a fortunate chance, Britain began a long-planned mobilization of her Second and Third Fleets which joined the First for a Royal Review at Spithead before carrying out exercises in the Channel. These included all her dreadnoughts—20 battleships and nine battlecruisers—except for three battlecruisers in the Mediterranean to counter the *Goeben* (the French had built none which could catch her) and the *Australia* in the South Pacific. Yet war was still believed to be so remote on 23rd July that the Second and Third Fleets returned to Chatham, Portsmouth and Devonport, their reservist crews being discharged to their homes. The nations of Europe were, however, already hastening towards the abyss. The heir to the Austro-Hungarian throne had been assassinated on 28th June whilst a British squadron was at Kiel for the reopening of the widened canal.

Counting on German support and supposing the outcome would be as advantageous as their rape of Bosnia and Herzegovina, the Austrian Government attributed this to Serbian intrigue and presented an ultimatum to Belgrade, whence an appeal went to St Petersburg for help in resisting terms so humiliating that no independent state could be expected to accept them. Nonetheless Berlin saw so little danger in the situation that the High Seas Fleet sailed on 7th July for its usual visit to Norwegian waters. The French viewed matters with equal unconcern; on 13th July the President left for the Baltic to visit the Tsar. And as late as 25th July Vienna had so far extended her time limit that it was confidently supposed that the storm would blow over. But the news which reached Whitehall next morning was so disturbing that Battenberg decided to cancel the First Fleet's summer leave and ordered the crews for the Second Fleet to be held ready to man their ships. Twenty-four hours later his fears were realized: Austria declared war and Berlin recalled the High Seas Fleet to the Jade.

> I have just heard from your Captain [of H.M.S. *Collingwood*] that all leave is stopped on account of the European situation and he has asked me for my instructions concerning your coming on leave on Friday as arranged. I have answered that of course you could not have leave until the situation has become normal again.

But there was to be no summer leave for Midshipman Prince Albert or any other officer or man in the British Fleet. On the same day, 28th July, that King George V wrote these lines to his second son, the Tsar ordered general mobilization in support of Serbia. This was enough for the Admiralty, which expected a surprise attack such as that with which the Japanese had launched their assault on Port Arthur, to take precautions before the Cabinet would authorize any of the other measures laid down in the War Book.

> We left Portland at 7 p.m. [Midshipman Prince Albert wrote] and steered west, and then east. The Captain gave us our war stations before lunch. We started war routine at 1 p.m. We were all in three watches, the control officers, searchlight officers, etc. After dinner we went to night defence stations. The 4-inch guns were all ready for a destroyer attack. We passed the Straits of Dover at midnight.

'We may picture this great Fleet, 18 miles of warships running at high speed and in absolute darkness through the Narrow Straits, bearing with them into the broad waters of the North the safeguard of considerable affairs' (*Churchill*). Whilst the Second Fleet, composed of less valuable pre-dreadnoughts, took the First's place at Portland, the Kaiser made a clumsy attempt to persuade the Tsar to countermand his order; then, on 1st August, declared war on Russia. He followed this by declaring war on France on the pretext that Germany's safety was threatened. Grey, scorning Chancellor Bethmann-Hollweg's suggestion that Britain should leave France to the mercy of her enemies, promptly told the French Ambassador that, 'if the German Fleet comes into the Channel or through the North Sea to undertake hostile operations against French coasts or shipping, the British Fleet will give all the protection in its power'. But before there was any call to fulfil this promise, the German Army advanced on France through the Ardennes and obliged the British Government to honour their guarantee of Belgium's neutrality. When there was no reply to an ultimatum which expired at 11 p.m. G.M.T. on 4th August, 'the war telegram which meant "Commence hostilities against Germany" was flashed to the ships and establishments under the White Ensign all over the world' (*Churchill*).

Britain's *casus belli* was Germany's decision to violate Belgium in the confident belief that her massive army would conquer France as quickly as it had done four decades before, but the root of her involvement lay in the Kaiser's *Weltpolitik* and his consequent decision to challenge British supremacy at sea. The circumstances in which Britain was drawn into the First World War are not, however, the main purpose of this chapter. More relevant to the Battle of Jutland is the rapidity with which the British Navy was jerked out of the Victorian complacency engendered by nearly a century of unchallenged supremacy, and made ready to face a new and undoubtedly efficient fleet whose creation had been unhindered by the weight of established tradition. As important are the material developments which dominated naval thought in the decade preceding the battle, in particular the evolution of the dreadnought battleship and the importance which Britain attached to having a considerably superiority over Germany in this type of vessel. For both factors were reflected in the strategy and tactics of the opposing fleets.

2

The Long Vigil

'At this grave moment in our national history I send to you, and through you to the officers and men of the fleet of which you have assumed command, the assurance of my confidence that, under your direction, they will revive and renew the old glories of the Royal Navy and prove once again the sure shield of Britain and her Empire in the hour of trial.'

King George V to Jellicoe, 5th August 1914

'At the outbreak of war, I was a midshipman keeping the middle watch on the bridge of H.M.S. *Collingwood* somewhere in the North Sea. I was 18 years of age. In the Grand Fleet everyone was pleased it had come at last. We had been trained in the belief that war between Germany and this country had to come one day, and when it did come we thought we were prepared for it.'

King George VI in his diary

ON 1ST AUGUST 1914, the British Home Fleet was under the command of the 62-year-old Admiral Callaghan whose three-year tenure was not due to expire until the end of the year. On the 2nd, however, Vice-Admiral Sir John Jellicoe, then 55, reached Scapa Flow, ostensibly to become Callaghan's Second-in-Command, but knowing that 'in certain circumstances [he] might be appointed Commander-in-Chief'. Before being relieved as Second Sea Lord he had 'protested [to Churchill and Battenberg] against such an appointment being made on what might be the eve of war', and soon after his arrival at Scapa he signalled the First Lord: 'Feel it my duty to warn you emphatically that you court disaster if you carry out [your] intention. Fleet is imbued with extreme admiration and loyalty for Commander-in-Chief.' But the Admiralty was adamant: 'we were doubtful as to Sir George Callaghan's health and physical strength being equal to the immense strain that would be cast upon him' (*Churchill*). Very early on 4th August Jellicoe was ordered to open a sealed envelope containing his appointment as Commander-in-Chief Grand Fleet, the Admiralty having decided to revive this historic title for the great force assembled in the Flow. 'I proceeded at once onboard the *Iron Duke* [where] a telegram having been received ordering the fleet to sea, Sir George arranged to leave before its departure at 0830.* At that hour I took over command.'

The son of a master mariner, John Rushworth Jellicoe joined the *Britannia* in 1874. Four years later he saw active service as a midshipman in the fleet which forced the Dardanelles. Three years more and he displayed high courage ashore after the bombardment of Alexandria where he conveyed dispatches through a horde of hostile *fellaheen*. The brilliance with which he qualified as a gunnery specialist brought him to Fisher's attention; when the latter became Director of Naval Ordnance, Jellicoe joined his staff at the Admiralty. In 1893 he chanced to be sick with Malta fever onboard the *Victoria* when she was rammed by the *Camperdown*, but he managed to take to the water before Tryon's flagship sank. The niche which Jellicoe had carved for himself was recognized in 1897 by his promotion to captain at the age of 35. In command of the flagship in China the toughness of his constitution was again tested; he was dangerously wounded during the Boxer rising. Next he was one of the small band of officers who helped Fisher prepare his momentous Memorandum, and, when the latter became First Sea Lord, Jellicoe became Director of Naval Ordnance, his gunnery experience enabling him to make an important contribution to the *Dreadnought* and *Invincible* designs. In 1907, he flew his flag as Rear-Admiral Second-in-Command of the Atlantic Fleet. Eighteen months later he became Third Sea Lord when he did much to maintain Britain's dreadnought lead over Germany. He could not, however, persuade Fisher to fight for bigger dry docks so that the new battleships might be built with the beam needed for an adequate weight of armour. Nor, with as much significance to the future, did he remain long enough at the Admiralty to ensure the design and provision of effective armour-piercing shell. When Fisher left the Admiralty, Jellicoe went back to sea in command of the Atlantic Fleet, whence he was transferred to the

---

* The 24-hour clock is used in this book to avoid confusion between a.m. and p.m. Times have been altered accordingly in quotations from other sources. Those in German accounts have been retarded two hours to conform with the British use of G.M.T.

1 *Commander-in-Chief of the British Grand Fleet: Admiral Sir John Jellicoe*

2 'Fear God and Dread Nought':
Vice-Admiral Sir John Fisher,
in 1897

3 Creator of the German High Seas
Fleet: Admiral Alfred von Tirpitz

Home Fleet's Second Division to gain experience with a squadron of dreadnoughts and to confirm his ability as a tactical commander. One year more and he became Second Sea Lord.

So much for Jellicoe's career, with its evidence of the outstanding talents and ability that led Fisher to cast him for the role of 'Admiralissimo when Armageddon comes'. Of the man himself Alfred Noyes wrote:

> The weatherwise face that showed no ageing sign
> But only grew in kindness year by year
> The shrewd brown twinkling eyes, the gentle heart,
> The resolute truth in judgment and in act . . .

What he lacked in physical stature was more than compensated by his strong and selfless character. He had deep religious convictions. Though his modesty prevented him carrying conviction much beyond the Fleet—Haig thought him 'an old woman'—he inspired admiration in those under his command to whom he was known as 'Silent Jack'. Few disputed that the Royal Navy had found the best available commander for its principal fleet, but Fisher was wrong when he wrote that 'he will be Nelson at Cape St Vincent until he becomes boss at Trafalgar when Armageddon comes', because Jellicoe had 'all the Nelsonic virtues save one'; notwithstanding his experience of a disaster resulting from blind obedience to orders, namely the loss of the *Victoria*, he was 'totally lacking in the great gift of insubordination'. He was a splendid administrator but his precise brain made such a cold analysis of each problem that he tended to reach the more cautious solution. He knew little of naval history: the 'Nelson touch' eluded him.

To the 20 dreadnought battleships which formed the core of the Grand Fleet when Jellicoe hoisted his flag in the *Iron Duke*, two more which had been about to commission for the Turkish Navy were soon added, increasing its margin to eight over Germany's 14. But since the latter had some 20 pre-dreadnoughts the Admiralty augmented Jellicoe's force with eight of the 'King Edward VII' class. The Grand Fleet was also considerably superior to the High Seas Fleet in cruisers and destroyers.* More important, to oppose Germany's five battle-

* Since the German Navy used the older classification of 'torpedoboat', this is used throughout this book for German vessels, both to facilitate distinction between the opposing flotillas and to emphasize the Germans' superior torpedo armament in contrast to the British 'destroyers' greater gunpower (*see Appendices I and II*).

cruisers (including the hybrid *Blücher*), Jellicoe had a squadron of five battlecruisers, of which the *Lion* flew the flag of Vice-Admiral Sir David Beatty. Twelve years younger than his Commander-in-Chief, and of hard-riding, hard-fighting, Irish stock, Beatty had gained the D.S.O. for leadership and courage under fire on the Nile in 1896. He was also promoted to commander's rank at the early age of 27. Like Jellicoe he was wounded in China during the Boxer troubles. For this service Beatty was promoted captain at 29 when the average age was 43; but though he commanded four cruisers and the battleship *Queen*, he spent so much time recovering from his wounds, in addition to two years as Naval Adviser to the Army Council, that he reached the top of the list without the sea service for flag rank. Fisher swept this obstacle aside in 1910; shortly before Beatty's thirty-ninth birthday, and only a few months later than Nelson first hoisted his flag, he was promoted rear-admiral by a special Order in Council. Yet he cared so little for this mark of Their Lordships' favour that he rejected an appointment as Second-in-Command of the Atlantic Fleet: he wanted a more independent command. The Board decided that he should not be offered further employment.

Fortunately Beatty met Churchill before he had completed the three years on half-pay which would have enforced his retirement, and the First Lord invited him to become his Naval Secretary. During the next fifteen months it became increasingly clear to Churchill that Beatty

> viewed naval strategy and tactics in a different light from the average naval officer. He did not think of *matériel* as an end in itself but only as a means. He thought of war problems in their unity by land, sea and air. [Unlike Jellicoe he was a keen student of naval history, especially the works of Mahan.] His mind had been rendered quick and supple by the situations of polo and the hunting field and enriched by varied experiences against the enemy. I had no doubts whatever, when the command of the Battlecruiser Squadron fell vacant in the spring of 1913, in appointing him over the heads of all to this incomparable command.

The First Lord's action did not endear Beatty to the Fleet; some officers never overcame their resentment. Yet he had not been in the *Lion* for many months before he proved that he could lead his squadron with all the dash that characterized him in the saddle, though he was sometimes prone to 'rush his fences'. Of robust physique and with a bulldog thrust to his jaw, he had the extrovert *panache* which Jellicoe lacked, but which was to endear him to his own officers and men as much as it helped the Press to build his public image. The rakish angle of his cap, his unorthodox six-buttoned monkey-jacket and his bull-dog 'Brindle Boy', also uniformed by Messrs Gieves, became as well known as Montgomery's battledress and beret twenty-five years later. But though the antithesis of his Commander-in-Chief there was no discord between them; Beatty might chafe so strongly against the Admiralty's authority as to earn from Churchill the tart rebuke: 'You must not continue to try to reverse decisions which have been taken with full knowledge of the circumstances and every desire if possible to meet your views' (*Signal dated 26th October 1914*), but for Jellicoe, who rode him on the lightest of reins, he showed nothing but the respect and loyalty proper to a subordinate flag officer. '*Beatty triomphe au polo. Jellicoe préfère le tennis*', wrote a Frenchman; before venturing so facile a comparison he should have remembered that it was the Dauphin's contempt for Henry V's addiction to tennis which led the English king to the field of Agincourt.

If two such notable admirals were chosen for the principal commands in the Grand Fleet, why did nearly two years elapse before it met the High Seas Fleet in battle? Howard and Drake waited in Plymouth Sound for the Armada to come up Channel; 150 years later Vernon and Anson conceived the more effective strategy of close blockade; since sailing ships-of-the-line could keep the sea for months on end, the British Fleet could best maintain command of the sea by lying close off an enemy's ports so that few ships escaped. Hawke sealed Conflans in Brest and Boscawen kept De la Clue in Toulon whilst Saunders carried Wolfe to Quebec; Cornwallis and Nelson confined Ganteaume, Latouche-Tréville and Villeneuve to the same ports so that Napoleon's *Grande Armée* never crossed the Channel. Such a close blockade was not, however, possible with coal-fired ironclads which only carried fuel for a few days at sea, as the Admiralty realized in the few years immediately preceding August 1914 when considering how best to deal with an enemy who faced them across the North Sea, instead of the English Channel, for the first time since the Dutch Wars. Minefields laid to seaward of enemy harbours made the task too dangerous: Togo had lost a third of his battleship strength off Port Arthur in May 1904. And the risk had been increased by submarines which could lurk unseen and sink a battleship with a single torpedo; there was no method of detecting these craft except for the chance sighting of a periscope, no defence except speed, zigzagging and the physical presence of a destroyer screen, and no way of sinking them except by ramming or gunfire. (Although hydrophones and depth-charges came into use before 1918, the Asdic—now Sonar—method of locating submerged submarines was not developed until after the First World War.)

After the Agadir crisis Bridgeman and Battenberg evolved a new strategy of *distant* blockade. The High Seas Fleet would be confined to the North Sea by a British fleet poised in some northern harbour, ready to weigh anchor whenever patrolling submarines reported that German ships had sailed. A force of light cruisers and destroyers, under Beatty's contemporary, Commodore Reginald Tyrwhitt, would be stationed at Harwich to keep the Narrow Seas (the area south of a line Flamborough Head–Heligoland) clear of enemy light craft and mine-layers. And 17 pre-dreadnoughts would be deployed in the Channel to close the Straits of Dover. The Firth of Forth and the Humber were best placed to serve as bases for the main fleet but there had been insufficient time to protect these anchorages from mines and submarines; Scapa Flow, which was believed to be beyond the range of Germany's U-boats, was therefore chosen.

Whilst blockade is the proper strategy for the stronger navy, the ultimate aim is to bring the enemy fleet to battle and destroy it. When Nelson triumphed at Trafalgar he must have remembered that Hawke had achieved as much when a gale drove him to the safety of Torbay and Conflans slipped out of Brest to be annihilated in Quiberon Bay. The Admiralty hoped for a like result in August 1914 since Tirpitz had so often boasted that the High Seas Fleet had been built to meet the British in combat and humble its paramount power. On the 4th Jellicoe was ordered to take the Grand Fleet out of Scapa for the first of a series of sweeps across the North Sea, returning to Scapa only for the short time necessary to coal, in part to paralyse German maritime trade and to ensure freedom of movement for British merchant shipping, but also in the belief that the High Seas Fleet would emerge for an attempt to stop the British Expeditionary Force crossing the Channel. But September came without the German battle fleet leaving Wilhelmshaven for reasons which had little to do with the efficiency of the British blockade.

Tirpitz might have the most bellicose intentions but his authority was limited. Since 1889 the German Admiralty had been divided into three bureaux whose heads were individually responsible to the Kaiser as Supreme War Lord. The Secretary of the Navy and his *Reich-marineamt* were limited matters of policy and material: Tirpitz had no control over operations; these were the responsibility of the *Admiralstab* which was headed by Admiral von Pohl who, like Jellicoe and Beatty, had made his mark during the Boxer Rebellion.* And this weak-willed officer was chiefly concerned to avoid displeasing his Imperial Master, who styled himself Admiral of the Atlantic but had been bred a soldier with a Continental mind so that he had as little understanding of sea power as Napoleon. In the confident hope that Paris would quickly fall to his unconquered Army, he was opposed to hazarding his Navy against a Fleet which 'had the advantage of looking back over a hundred years of proud tradition which must have given every man a sense of superiority based on the great deeds of the past' (*Scheer*). Hence the Kaiser's Imperial Order of July 1914 which only allowed the High Seas Fleet to go beyond a line from the Horn Reefs to Terschelling 'if a favourable opportunity to strike offers itself'. Otherwise it was to wage no more than 'guerrilla warfare against the English until we had achieved such a weakening of their fleet that we could safely send out our own' (*Tirpitz*). But an inferiority complex was not the sole reason for the Kaiser's insistence on a 'fleet in being', however much he might share Mahan's admiration for the skilful way in which the French had used this strategy to weaken British superior strength during the eighteenth century. The German High Command supposed that the British Navy would attempt a *close* blockade which would enable them to reduce its superiority by mines and torpedoes. They also believed that the High Seas Fleet should be conserved to defeat a British attempt to land an army on their North Sea coast.

So the German battle fleet remained in the Jade whilst the British Expeditionary Force crossed the Channel without the loss of a single man. Enemy light craft did, however, make two sorties across the southern North Sea on 21st and 23rd August, which inspired the Admiralty to order Tyrwhitt to take his ships into the Bight at dawn on the 28th. The Germans met him with a stronger force than he expected—seven light cruisers and two flotillas of torpedoboats—and his flagship was seriously damaged. Fortunately Jellicoe had ordered

* The third bureau was the *Marinekabinett*, responsible for the training and appointment of officers, whose head, Admiral von Müller, was also a member of the Kaiser's Court.

his Battlecruiser Squadron and six light cruisers south in support. Taking the calculated risk of mines, U-boats and a possible sortie by the enemy battle fleet, Beatty sped to the *Arethusa*'s rescue and, using his heavy guns with devastating effect at short range in low visibility, quickly sank the light cruisers *Ariadne, Köln and Mainz* and enabled Tyrwhitt to withdraw. This defeat, 'fateful both in its after-effects and incidental results for the work of our Navy' (*Tirpitz*), confirmed the Kaiser in his decision not to hazard his Fleet. Although the 'Miracle of the Marne' put paid to his expectations of an early victory on land, he amplified his restrictive instructions to the Fleet which was 'to hold itself back and avoid actions which can lead to greater losses'.

Paradoxically, this action was evidence to Jellicoe that the fighting qualities of the German Army had been inherited by the High Seas Fleet. But since it showed no inclination to challenge his command of the North Sea, he had a more pressing worry: as early as 9th August he had evidence that German submarines could operate in the northern North Sea, and on 1st September one was reported inside Scapa Flow. Though subsequent investigation dismissed this as false, Jellicoe was satisfied that, contrary to the Admiralty's intelligence, the Orkneys were within U-boat range. Until urgent measures to strengthen Scapa's defences could be completed, he was compelled to use Loch Ewe for coaling and, when a U-boat was reported there on 7th October, to move to Lough Swilly. This was so far from the North Sea, where the High Seas Fleet was now expected to make a sortie in support of a German attempt to land troops on the British east coast, that Jellicoe was compelled to keep his fleet almost continuously at sea with the consequence that it could not be maintained at its full strength. His opponent, Admiral von Ingenohl, a competent but uninspired leader, could plan to have all his 16 dreadnoughts and five battlecruisers (by the end of October) available on a chosen day. But ships required to spend all their time at sea, with never longer than 24 hours in harbour for coaling, become increasingly subject to engine defects. Moreover, with the prospect of a longer war than anyone (except Lord Kitchener) had envisaged, refits could not be deferred. For both these reasons as many as four of Jellicoe's 23 dreadnoughts and seven battlecruisers (at the end of October) might be in dockyard hands. Damage by grounding or collision, as happened between the *Monarch* and *Conqueror*, might deprive him of two more. There was also the danger of losses by submarine attack and mines: the latter accounted for the dreadnought *Audacious* on 27th October. And so long as there were enemy cruisers abroad the Admiralty might have to deploy battlecruisers to counter them; they used one to protect a Canadian troop convoy across the Northern Atlantic and, after Cradock's defeat at Coronel on 8th November, dispatched the *Invincible* and *Inflexible* to the Falklands and the *Princess Royal* to the Caribbean. All these factors led Jellicoe to the disturbing conclusion that the Grand Fleet might have little or no dreadnought margin when it encountered the High Seas Fleet.

This prompted him to write to the Admiralty on 30th October:

> The experience gained of German methods since the commencement of the war makes it possible and very desirable to consider the manner in which [they] are likely to be made use of tactically in a fleet action. The Germans have shown that they rely to a very great extent on submarines, mines and torpedoes, and there can be no doubt whatever that they will endeavour to make the fullest use of these weapons in a fleet action, especially since they possess an actual superiority over us in these particular directions.* [However they] cannot rely with certainty upon having their full complement of submarines and minelayers present in a fleet action unless the battle is fought in the southern area of the North Sea. *My object will therefore be to fight the fleet action in the northern portion of the North Sea.*†

In short, there would be no battle between the Grand Fleet and the High Seas Fleet unless the latter ventured further into the North Sea than, unknown to the Admiralty or Jellicoe, the Kaiser had any intention of permitting. Jellicoe's strategical conclusion was paralleled by his ideas on tactics; the use of submarines with the German Battle Fleet

> can be countered by judicious handling of our Battle Fleet, but may, and probably will, involve a refusal to comply with the enemy's tactics by moving in the invited direction. If, for instance, the enemy Battle Fleet were to turn *away* from an advancing fleet, I should assume that the intention was to lead us over mines and submarines, and should *decline to be so drawn*. I desire particularly to draw the attention of Their Lordships to this point since it may be deemed a refusal of battle and, indeed, might possibly result *in failure to bring an enemy to action* as soon as is expected and hoped. Such a result would be absolutely repugnant to the feelings of all British naval officers and men, but with new and

* Jellicoe knew this from more than experience; he had a translation of the German Navy's battle orders which were captured by the Russians from the *Magdeburg* (*vide* p. 43).

† Author's italics.

untried methods of warfare new tactics must be devised to meet them. I feel that such tactics, if not understood, may bring odium upon me, but it is quite within the bounds of possibility that *half our Battle Fleet might be disabled by underwater attack before the guns opened fire at all.* The safeguard against submarines will consist in moving the Battle Fleet at very high speed to a flank before deployment takes place or the gun action commences. This will take us off the ground on which the enemy desires to fight, but it may, of course, result in a refusal to follow me. But *if the Battle Fleets remain in sight of one another*, I should feel that after an interval of high-speed manœuvring I could safely close.*

Jellicoe showed considerable moral courage when he submitted such cautious ideas to an Admiralty now headed by two men so offensively minded as Churchill and Fisher. But if he had studied history he would have known that British naval superiority was not achieved by material might. Hawke wrote: 'It is a matter of indifference whether I fight the enemy with an equal number, one ship more, or one less.' Other British admirals have defeated superior fleets: Jervis at St Vincent had only 15 sail-of-the-line against Spain's 27. 'The superiority in the number of ships on which Great Britain today relies for her safety and superiority, was not the decisive factor', wrote the German Vice-Admiral Livonius in 1902; 'it was the genius of her captains and admirals which produced Britain's glorious victories.' Nor could Jellicoe claim that steam and steel had reduced the importance of the human factor, since Togo's genius had enabled four battleships, supported by eight cruisers, to annihilate a Russian force of eight battleships and four cruisers at Tsushima. It is true that, after his initial serious losses off Port Arthur and prior to this battle, Togo's strategy was as cautious as Jellicoe's; but Japan had no shipbuilding industry to provide further vessels whereas Jellicoe could expect 14 more dreadnoughts in the course of the next two years against only five on German slips.

However, notwithstanding these lessons and the objections of Wilson (recalled at the outbreak of war to assist the First Sea Lord) who pointed out the tactical difficulties of operating submarines with a fleet, the Admiralty gave Jellicoe their unqualified approval on 7th November, assuring him 'of their full confidence in your contemplated conduct of the Fleet in action'. They added that, if a fleet action appeared imminent, all available forces not attached to the Grand Fleet would be ordered out in support, although Admiral Sir Henry Jackson, who had also

* Author's italics.

been recalled to the Admiralty at the outbreak of war, had strong reservations against committing the Harwich Force in this way. Since Churchill and Fisher were students of history as well as believers in the offensive—'rashness in war is prudence, as prudence in war is criminal' (*Fisher*)—why did they agree to a policy which contradicted both? Fisher was much occupied with a scheme for ending the deadlock in Flanders which had captured Churchill's imagination; they were planning a special armada of more than 600 vessels to land an army on the German Baltic coast only 90 miles from Berlin. And there was no effective Admiralty War Staff to advise them otherwise. In the 19 months which were to elapse before Jutland the Baltic project was superseded by a wiser but ill-executed amphibious assault on the enemy's other flank, the Dardanelles, which led to both the First Lord and First Sea Lord being superseded by Balfour and Jackson in May 1915. Yet neither the Admiralty nor Jellicoe amended their ideas of how the Grand Fleet should be employed even when its numerical superiority increased considerably after the latter part of 1915. 'I take the fullest responsibility for approving the answer proposed by the First Sea Lord. There was no reason in the first phase of the naval war for seeking a battle except in the best conditions', wrote Churchill. 'But I do not accept any responsibility for the actual conduct of an operation [Jutland] which took place 18 months later in conditions of relative strength different from those which existed in October 1914.'*

Whilst comment on Jellicoe's tactics, and upon his startling suggestion that half his fleet might be disabled before action was joined, is best reserved until the story of Jutland is told, it can be said now that his intention not to be drawn into the southern portion of the North Sea was justified. Such caution may not have been in accord with tradition, but no previous British admiral had had to contend with such potentially dangerous hazards as the mine and the submarine. Though the superior navy's ultimate aim should be destruction of the enemy, this is not to be sought without regard for the consequences of failure, since this could involve inability to maintain the principal strategic object, to command the sea by blockade. 'The British battle fleet is like the queen on the chess board; it may remain at the base but

---

* Not quite accurate; on 5th April 1915, Jellicoe submitted similar views to those of 30th October 1914, which the Admiralty again approved. However, Jackson seems to have been ignorant of the existence of both letters until some two and a half months after Jutland.

it still dominates the game. It is the final arbiter at sea; to lose it is to lose the game' (*Chatfield*). In Churchill's words, 'the destruction of the British Battle Fleet was final'; Jellicoe was 'the only man on either side who could lose the war in an afternoon'. As important, the reverse of Churchill's comment, that Jellicoe was in a position to *win* the war in an afternoon, was never true. A decisively defeated High Seas Fleet would have done no more to weaken the German Army's stranglehold on Europe than Trafalgar weakened Napoleon's, though it would have released ships of the Grand Fleet for other operations, notably des-troyers to combat the U-boat campaign, and squadrons to operate in the Baltic in conjunction with the Russian Fleet, especially against the Swedish iron ore traffic which came down the Gulf of Bothnia. In the words of Jellicoe's opponent, Admiral Scheer, written shortly *after* Jutland: 'There can be no doubt that even the most favourable issue [to Germany] of a battle on the high seas will not compel England to make peace in this war. The disadvantages of our geographical position compared with that of the Island Empire and her great material superiority cannot be compensated for by our Fleet.'

Jellicoe's caution, combined with the Kaiser's restrictions on his Fleet, thus did much to delay a major clash for two years; there was, however, a number of other engagements. On 17th October 1914, four German torpedoboats were wiped out by a small British force whilst attempting to lay mines off the Thames Estuary. Ascribing this disaster to instruc-tions which prevented him supporting his light forces, Ingenohl, who was also concerned with the moral effect of inactivity on his ships' crews, pressed to be allowed to carry out a retaliatory operation. The High Command repeated that 'the fleet must be held back and avoid action which might lead to heavy losses', but 'there is nothing to be said against an attempt of the big cruisers to damage the enemy.' The German Commander-in-Chief responded by sending his battlecruisers to bombard Yarmouth on 3rd November. This fishing port was too far south for the Grand Fleet to reach the scene in time, whilst Tyrwhitt's attempt to cut off the enemy before they reached the Jade was un-successful. Nonetheless the Germans lost the cruiser *Yorck* on a mine as she was returning to harbour.

There were two developments before Ingenohl could repeat this raid. Beatty's battlecruisers were moved south to Cromarty and Bradford's Third Battle Squadron (of 'King Edward VIIs') to Rosyth.

The Admiralty also developed a new source of intelligence. Since submarines patrolling the Heligoland Bight were not a reliable substitute for the frigates which Hawke and Nelson had stationed off Brest and Cadiz to give timely warning of the enemy leaving port, a chain of direction-finding stations had been erected to locate enemy warships by their wireless transmissions. The bearings which these provided were supplemented by a much more fruitful method after the cruiser *Magdeburg* was wrecked in the Gulf of Finland on 27th August; the Russians salvaged her copies of the German Navy's codes and sent them to London, and by December a specially recruited team working in Room 40OB (Old Building) at the Admiralty under Sir Alfred Ewing, was able to decipher enough German signals to give advance warning of sorties by the High Seas Fleet: in particular that the German battlecruisers were to raid the Yorkshire coast at dawn on the 16th.

This time Ingenohl's purpose was more than retaliatory; the Falkland Islands battle had told him that two of Beatty's battlecruisers were in the Atlantic; the opportunity to inflict damage on a weakened Grand Fleet was not to be missed. Room 40 failed, however, to glean the news that Ingenohl intended to bring out his whole fleet. So the Admiralty—which tended to usurp the Commander-in-Chief's role by ordering him to send particular units, sometimes to specified positions, to counter enemy moves instead of giving him all available intelligence and leaving him to act on it—instructed Jellicoe to send no more than Warrender's Second Battle Squadron and Pakenham's Third Cruiser Squadron south in support of Beatty's four battlecruisers, Goodenough's First Light Cruiser Squadron and Tyrwhitt's Harwich Force. In the event, the German battle fleet's sortie was of no consequence. Though Beatty's destroyers made chance contact with Ingenohl's torpedoboats to the south of the Dogger Bank shortly before dawn, the British Admiral was deterred by poor visibility, coupled with positive reports that German heavy ships were off the Yorkshire coast, from pursuit of what could be no more than a detached flotilla. And the German Commander-in-Chief, being as ready to believe that he was about to run into the Grand Fleet as he was fearful of the All Highest's wrath, promptly returned to the Jade, unmindful of the extent to which this would turn the snare he had planned into a trap for his battlecruisers. For, whilst the cruiser *Kolberg* laid a minefield, the *Derfflinger* and *Von der Tann* fired on the undefended seaside resorts of

Scarborough and Whitby, and the *Seydlitz*, *Molke* and *Blücher* inflicted greater damage on the port of Hartlepool, their three escape routes through the minefields off the east coast were blocked, to the south by Warrender and Tyrwhitt, in the centre by Beatty, and to the north by Bradford from Rosyth. Choosing the centre gap for their retirement, the German ships were sighted shortly before noon, despite worsening weather, by Goodenough in the *Southampton*, wing ship of a light cruiser screen ahead of the British battlecruisers. The *Birmingham*, *Nottingham* and *Falmouth* swung round to support their Commodore. Intending to limit this movement to the *Birmingham*, Beatty signalled the other two ships to resume station. Unfortunately his message was passed to all four so that the *Southampton* and *Birmingham*, which reluctantly complied, lost touch with the enemy. A little later the *Orion*, Captain F. C. Dreyer, flying the flag of Rear-Admiral Sir Robert Arbuthnot, second-in-command of Warrender's squadron, sighted Hipper's light cruisers and destroyers. 'I [Dreyer] put our guns on the leading light cruisers, and asked Sir Robert's permission to open fire, but he said, "No, not until the Vice-Admiral [Warrender] signals 'open fire', or his flagship fires." He never spoke to me about it afterwards but I am certain he was mortified to realize that he had been too punctilious. The German force had hauled away to the northward [before Warrender saw them] and our golden moment had been missed.' Four factors thus combined to enable the German battlecruisers to slip through the British net: typical North Sea weather, a signal error, Goodenough's tactical mistake and Arbuthnot's lack of initiative consequent on the British Navy's concept of superior orders. On Beatty they 'left a mark which nothing can eradicate except total destruction of the enemy. We were within an ace of accomplishing it. Our advanced ships had sighted them! I can't bear to write about it'. Meanwhile public indignation at the German breach of the Hague Convention led the Admiralty to move the British battlecruisers south to Rosyth where they would be better placed to intercept a further raid.

Allowing for ships completed since the outbreak of war, absent abroad and undergoing repairs or refitting, Jellicoe's margin of strength over Ingenohl was now very small: five battlecruisers against four plus the *Blücher*, and 18 dreadnoughts plus eight pre-dreadnoughts against a possible 17 dreadnoughts and up to 22 older battleships. Ingenohl therefore planned another sortie in January 1915: four light cruisers and a torpedoboat flotilla, supported by three battlecruisers and the *Blücher*, were ordered to raid the British Dogger Bank fishing fleet on the 24th. Room 40 gave enough warning for the Admiralty to order Beatty, Bradford, Pakenham, Goodenough and Tyrwhitt to sail with their squadrons on the previous evening, whilst Jellicoe brought his battle fleet south from Scapa in support. At dawn the *Lion*, leading the *Tiger*, *Princess Royal*, *New Zealand*, flying the flag of Beatty's second-in-command, Rear-Admiral Sir Archibald Moore, and *Indomitable*, had just made their appointed rendezvous with the *Arethusa* on the north-east part of the Dogger Bank, when the *Aurora*, 12 miles to the south of Tyrwhitt's flagship, reported that she was in action with the *Kolberg*. The Germans reacted to this unexpected contact by assuming the presence of a superior force and heading for home at high speed. But they could not elude Goodenough: determined to retrieve his recent mistake, the Commodore pressed on to report the enemy battlecruisers at 0730. This enabled Beatty to turn his squadron in pursuit; soon he had his opponent in sight for the first time since the outbreak of war. But it required an hour's stern chase to bring the *Lion* within gun range of the *Blücher* at the rear of the German line. Before long the *Tiger* and *Princess Royal* joined in against this under-gunned ship, to which the faster German battlecruisers gave no support until 0914 when the *Lion* was able to shift target to the *Moltke*.

By 0935 Beatty had gained enough on the enemy to order his squadron to engage their opposite numbers; he intended his three leading battle-cruisers to match the enemy's ship for ship, leaving the *Blücher* to the *New Zealand* and *Indomitable*. But the *Tiger*'s captain supposed he was meant to comply with a *Grand Fleet Battle Order* to the effect that, with five ships against four, two should concentrate on the leading enemy vessel. The *Tiger* joined the *Lion* in inflicting serious damage on the *Seydlitz*, and the *Moltke* was left unfired at for some 15 minutes whilst she concentrated with the other German vessels on Beatty's flagship. Between 1015 and 1030 salvoes penetrated the *Lion*'s side armour in two places and caused considerable flooding. Nonetheless, the chase continued at a speed which made it impracticable for either side's flotillas to execute a torpedo attack, and the *Blücher* dropped more and more behind until 1048 when she was observed to be out of control. Beatty ordered the *Indomitable* to finish her off. Before she could comply he signalled all his ships to make a 90-degree turn to port to avoid a U-boat. A few minutes later, realizing that so large an alteration of course would lose too much ground on a flying enemy, he hoisted

'Course NE' to limit the turn to 45 degrees. All five British battle-cruisers were then heading for the *Blücher* when a salvo inflicted so much damage to the *Lion*'s port engine-room that one engine had to be stopped. With her speed cut to 15 knots and a considerable list she dropped out of the line; but before Beatty lost all control of his squadron he issued two more orders, 'Attack the enemy's rear', followed by, 'Keep closer to the enemy'. Unhappily the first was hoisted with 'Course NE' still flying, whilst the distance separating the stricken flagship from the rest of her squadron had become too great for the second to be distinguished; so Beatty's last order was read as 'Attack the enemy's rear bearing NE'. This being the *Blücher*'s bearing, Moore understood that he was to deal with her; so did the *Tiger* and *Princess Royal* which joined with the *New Zealand* and *Indomitable* in completing the destruction of the Germans' lame duck. By the time she sank at 1210, after being hit by seven torpedoes in addition to more than 70 shells, the other three German battlecruisers, whose Admiral was chiefly concerned to save the crippled *Seydlitz*, were well over the horizon. When Beatty, having transferred by destroyer to the *Princess Royal*, was able to resume command of his force, he could do no more than escort the damaged *Lion* back to Rosyth in tow of the *Indomitable*.

'The sinking of the *Blücher* and the flight, after heavy injuries, of the other German ships was accepted as a solid and indisputable result', wrote Churchill. It was indeed a British victory, for which the credit was Beatty's, but it might well have been a more decisive one if he had not been deprived of control at a critical juncture by the damaged sustained by the *Lion*, and by Moore's subsequent decision to destroy one already crippled cruiser instead of continuing in pursuit of the main enemy force. He 'ought to have gone on, had he the slightest Nelsonic temperament in him, regardless of signals. In war the first principle is to disobey orders. Any fool can obey orders' (*Fisher*). But Beatty's second-in-command had been schooled in a navy which inculcated implicit obedience. Moreover Beatty had contributed to Moore's conduct: his signal, 'Attack the enemy's rear', was as unnecessary as it was open to misinterpretation. (Beatty wanted to signal, 'Engage the enemy more closely', but this Nelsonic injunction had been deleted from the signal book. Too late, his Signal Officer found the weak alternative, 'Keep closer to the enemy'.) For this reason he refrained from condemning Moore, leaving it to the Admiralty to remove him quietly from the Grand Fleet. But a court-martial would have done more to drive home the lesson that the Grand Fleet had lost a chance of inflicting a decisive defeat for the second time within two months through a flag officer's compliance with a superior order instead of using his own judgment. Again, too, there were signal mistakes. In contrast the Germans learned a vital lesson from their damaged flagship. The flash from cordite ignited by shells exploding in the *Seydlitz*'s two after gunhouses had passed down the turret trunks and, but for quick flooding, would have detonated the magazines. Steps to minimise this danger, from which the dreadnoughts of all navies suffered, were therefore taken in the High Seas Fleet before Jutland.

Shortly after this the Grand Fleet was reorganized. Increased to seven by ships recalled from overseas following the elimination of German cruisers from the trade routes, Beatty's battlecruisers were divided into two squadrons: with three light cruiser squadrons, including Goodenough's (renumbered the Second) and a force of destroyers, these formed the Battlecruiser Fleet based on Rosyth.* At the same time Jellicoe allowed one squadron of battleships to move south to Cromarty. And on 23rd March he wrote to Beatty a letter so percipient and of such prophetic importance as to justify quotation *in extenso*:

> I imagine that the Germans will sooner or later try to entrap you by risking [their] battlecruisers as a decoy. They must know that I am—where I am—and you are—where you are; and they may well argue that the position is one which lends itself to a trap to bring you into the High Seas Fleet, with the battlecruisers as bait. They know that if they can get you in chase, the odds are that you will be 100 miles away from me, and they can under such conditions draw you well down to the Heligoland Bight without my being in effective support. It is quite all right if you keep your speed, of course, but if you have some ships with their speed badly reduced in the fight with their battlecruisers, or by submarines, the loss of such ships seems inevitable if you are drawn into the vicinity of the High Seas Fleet with me too far off to get to your help, or their help, so as to extricate them before dark. A night action in the Heligoland Bight is unthinkable. The Germans might well get the High Seas Fleet so placed as to cut in behind you. Such a scheme is one

* The main body of the Grand Fleet, *i.e.* the battle squadrons, cruiser squadrons and destroyer flotillas which remained based on Scapa and Cromarty, was then known as the *Battle Fleet*. This distinction (*i.e.* the use of capital initial letters) is observed in this book for both sides. When spelled with small initial letters, the term *battle fleet* is limited to its normal collective meaning for several squadrons of battleships.

which we should certainly try if we were in the Germans' shoes. The Germans also probably know you and your qualities very well by report and will try to take advantage of that quality of 'not letting go when you have once got hold', which you possess, thank God. The Admiralty and the Country's attitude would certainly be one of great praise in case of success, and one of exactly the opposite should you have ill luck over such a venture. One need not worry about the attitude of others possibly, but one must concern oneself very seriously with the result to the Country of a piece of real bad luck culminating in a serious decrease in *relative* strength. Of course, the whole thing is a question of the game being worth the candle, and only the man on the spot can decide. If the game looks worth the candle the risks can well be taken. If not, then however distasteful, I think one's duty is to be cautious. I firmly believe you will see which is the proper course under the circumstances and that you will pursue it victoriously.

A year was, however, to elapse before the Germans set the trap of which Jellicoe thus warned his subordinate. For although by the end of 1915 the British battle fleet comprised 27 dreadnoughts (including three of the new oil-fired, 24-knot, 15-inch gunned 'Queen Elizabeth' class), whilst the German strength remained at 17, and Beatty's battle-cruisers were likewise increased to nine, divided into three squadrons, when the German four were augmented only by the *Lützow*, the High Seas Fleet had a new Commander-in-Chief. Irrationally angered by the loss of the *Blücher*, the Kaiser removed Ingenohl and replaced him by the complacent Pohl who, from February to December, limited his activities to occasional minelaying sorties. The German Battle Fleet went no further than the Horn Reefs, thereby avoiding a further encounter with Jellicoe's ships which added raids on the Skagerrak to their periodical sweeps across the North Sea. Admiral Bachmann, who was Pohl's successor at the *Admiralstab*, was involved in a very different offensive. Pohl had gained Tirpitz's support for using U-boats to strike a blow at British maritime trade against which the Grand Fleet would be no protection. Bethmann-Hollweg resolutely opposed this: he feared the reaction of neutrals to their ships being attacked contrary to International Law. Once again an impatient Supreme War Lord overruled a civilian Minister in favour of a Service adviser: from 16th February 1915, Germany declared a War Zone round the British Isles in which 'every merchant vessel found will be destroyed without its being always possible to avoid damage to the crews and passengers', it being 'impossible to avoid attacks being made on neutral ships in

4 Rear-Admiral Franz von Hipper,
Leader of the German Scouting Force

5 Vice-Admiral Reinhard Scheer,
Commander-in-Chief of the German
High Seas Fleet

6 *The Eyes of the Grand Fleet: Commodore W. E. Goodenough*

7 *Commander of the British Battle-cruiser Fleet: Vice-Admiral Sir David Beatty (after his promotion to Admiral)*

mistake for those of the enemy'. Bethmann-Hollweg's fears were soon realized: initial neutral objections were as nothing to those which followed the sinking of the British transatlantic liner *Lusitania* off Queenstown on 7th May with the loss of 1,198 lives; the world raised its voice in outraged protest at an act of inhumanity such as no civilized belligerent had previously dared perpetrate. The Kaiser compromised only to the extent of banning attacks on large passenger ships which made no offensive move; his U-boats were having too many successes against a nation whose war plans had rejected the need for convoys, for him to do more than this to pacify even so powerful a neutral as the United States. This was not enough to stop another serious 'incident'; whilst Washington was still arguing with Berlin on 19th August, *U24* chose to interpret a zigzag course by the White Star liner *Arabic* as an offensive manœuvre and sent her to the bottom of the Irish Sea. This time Washington's protest was so strong that Bethmann-Hollweg's counsel prevailed: Bachmann was superseded by Admiral von Holtzendorff, and on 5th October the order went out 'to cease all forms of submarine warfare on the west coast of Great Britain or in the Channel'. So much for Germany's first essay at unrestricted U-boat warfare.

> The deadly monotony of the work of the Grand Fleet will probably never be fully realized by any but those whose fate it was to wait day after day and week after week for the longed-for encounter with the enemy. Only that ever-present hope carried us through that dreary second winter of war. An occasional interval at sea for manœuvres was the sole relief, and such was our cussedness that even these were greeted by most of us with moans and groans, for we were reduced to a state of irritability and boredom which only the prospect of action or leave could mitigate.

So wrote a young officer in the battleship *Hercules*. With no greater complaint the Fleet, under Jellicoe's leadership, endured the barren wastes of Scapa Flow, with its frequent mists, its gales and its long winter nights, not to mention the toil and filth of coaling ship on returning to harbour from each trip to sea. Beatty's ships were more fortunate: Edinburgh was close to hand. So, too, were the officers and men of the High Seas Fleet in their anchorage near Wilhelmshaven; yet their morale was not to remain proof against boredom and inaction; in time they were to fall a prey to seditious propaganda and commit serious breaches of discipline. These did not, however, trouble Pohl, for in January 1916 he was found to be mortally ill with cancer and obliged to give up his command.

Vice-Admiral Reinhard Scheer who succeeded him was born four years later than Jellicoe. Entering the German Navy in 1882 with the handicap of a middle-class upbringing in a country which chose most of its officers from the wealthy land-owning families, his advancement was slow. Not until he commanded a torpedoboat flotilla in 1900 did he make his mark with a text-book on the tactical use of the torpedo. Thereafter his worth was recognized as captain of a battleship and, in 1912, as Chief of Staff in the High Seas Fleet. Just over 50 when war broke out, he first commanded the Second Battle Squadron, then the Third. Though neither was engaged with the enemy, 18 months' continuous war service in the High Seas Fleet qualified him for the supreme command. It is not, however, easy to understand why the Kaiser accepted him since he was amongst those who, like Tirpitz, had persistently pressed for the German Fleet to take the offensive; believing Germany's ships to be superior to the British, and German officers and men their equals, he refused to accept the argument that a numerically weaker fleet must suffer defeat. His unattractive features mirrored his strength of character as much as his simple personality. He might be lacking in imagination and a sense of humour but the High Seas Fleet, which was suffering the frustration of a year's inactivity, welcomed him as a vigorous leader with an established reputation as a tactician, who understood the importance of well-trained ships.

The man whom the Kaiser might have been expected to choose to follow Pohl was Rear-Admiral Franz Hipper. The same age as Scheer, and from the same middle-class stock, his promotion had been as slow. But by 1914 he had achieved command of the German Scouting Groups, in particular the battlecruisers. In these he had led the raid on the Yorkshire coast and fought at the Dogger Bank, proving his capacity to take the offensive whilst avoiding action with any substantial enemy force. Moreover, in addition to being an exceptionally able professional seaman with the ability to train his ships near to perfection, he had refused to take any part in the agitation for the High Seas Fleet to play a more aggressive role. Yet, though Scheer's equal as a tactician and a fighter, this tall, distinguished looking officer remained in command of the Scouting Groups, perhaps because his superiors could not believe that so quiet, so unassuming a personality could have the qualities needed to command a fleet.

Be this as it may, Scheer and Hipper were worthy opponents of Jellicoe and Beatty, matching them in talent, ability and experience, except that both suffered under a handicap as serious as the numerical inferiority of their fleet. The British Admirals came from the same stable as Grenville, Hawke and St Vincent. Jellicoe might err on the side of caution but he and Beatty were heirs to that fine quality which has so often enabled Britain's leaders to achieve what Drake called 'the true glory'. Keyes at Zeebrugge in 1918 and Cowan at Kronstadt a year later epitomized what Cunningham expressed so well at the time of the fall of Crete: a ship can be built in three years but it takes three centuries to build a tradition. Tirpitz's verdict, 'the German people have not understood the sea', may be an exaggeration in the light of the near-success of the U-boat campaign in 1917. But Spee's conduct off the Falkland Islands in December 1914 exemplifies the handicap under which all German admirals suffered because their Fleet was such a recent creation; he turned and fled, not from Sturdee's battlecruisers, but from what he first thought were old pre-dreadnoughts which the guns of his armoured cruisers could have destroyed in Port Stanley harbour before they had time to raise steam and slip their cables. In the same way Scheer and Hipper were handicapped by more than the Kaiser's restrictions on the High Seas Fleet: they were reluctant to fight a navy which enjoyed a centuries-old reputation of near invincibility.

The Admiralty, now headed by Jackson, realized that the High Seas Fleet had found a leader of different calibre to Pohl when German light forces successfully attacked a minesweeping flotilla near the Dogger Bank early in February 1916, and escaped before either Beatty or Tyrwhitt could reach the scene. In the same month Scheer's zeppelins intensified their raids on Britain. But neither of these activities satisfied Ludendorff's demands for a naval offensive which would oblige the Allies to relax their hold on the corpse-strewn slopes of Verdun. A note from the United States to all belligerents, dated 18th January 1916, seemed to present a solution. Although Asquith's Government quickly rejected its unhappy suggestion that merchant ships should no longer be armed for their own defence, so that Germany could have no excuse for resuming unrestricted U-boat warfare, Berlin supposed that Washington would adopt retaliatory measures to compel London's compliance and, by curiously tortuous thinking, that it would be safe to allow U-boats to operate throughout the War Zone provided that passenger ships were not attacked. This restriction was too much for the bellicose Tirpitz, 'the one German sailor who understands war' (Fisher), whose efforts to create the post of Supreme Commander of the

Navy for himself had failed to overcome the Kaiser's objections to relinquishing his supreme powers. Not for the first time he tendered his resignation and on this occasion it was accepted. Nemesis came quickly to his successor, Admiral von Capelle: on 24th March *UB29* torpedoed the cross-Channel steamer *Sussex*, carrying a number of American passengers, on the pretext that she was a troop transport. Three weeks later Washington notified Berlin that, unless Germany immediately abandoned 'submarine warfare against passengers and freight-carrying vessels, the Government of the United States can have no choice but to sever diplomatic relations with the German Empire'.

Compelled to decide between his Service advisers, who urged that only unrestricted U-boat warfare could bring much needed relief to the hard-pressed German Army, and Bethmann-Hollweg's assurance that this would force the United States into the war on the side of the Allies, the Kaiser compromised again. On 23rd February 1916, he authorized the alternative of cautious offensive operations by the High Seas Fleet designed to trap and overwhelm weaker elements of the Grand Fleet. Early in March Scheer supported a cruiser sortie with two squadrons of dreadnoughts, but without result; the Admiralty learned of it too late to order the Grand Fleet out. Ten days later the Harwich force escorted the seaplane-carrier *Vindex* across the North Sea for an air attack on the zeppelin sheds at Tondern, behind the island of Sylt. Tyrwhitt's retirement was delayed by a destroyer collision and, later, by a more serious one between the light cruiser *Undaunted* and his own flagship, now the *Cleopatra*. The Battlecruiser Fleet, followed by the British Battle Fleet, hurried to their rescue as the High Seas Fleet left the Jade intent on their destruction; and early on 26th March it seemed that Beatty would meet Scheer and Hipper before Jellicoe could reach the scene. But a full gale with mountainous seas decided Scheer against risking an engagement in unfavourable weather and he returned to harbour without being sighted.

The High Seas Fleet next put to sea on 21st April in the belief that Tyrwhitt was about to attack Tondern again. Room 40 gave enough warning of this move for the Grand Fleet to be ordered towards the Skagerrak. But before they could arrive early on the 22nd Scheer, whose intelligence sources never compared in efficiency with the Admiralty's, concluded that Tyrwhitt's attack had been put off and ordered his ships back to the Jade. Jellicoe held on towards the Horn Reefs hoping to draw him out; but that afternoon the British battlecruisers ran into a dense fog, and at 1800 the *Australia* and *New Zealand* were so badly damaged in collision that Beatty had to return to Rosyth. The British Battle Fleet had similar trouble: the dreadnought *Neptune* collided with a neutral merchant ship and three destroyers were likewise crippled, so that Jellicoe was back in Scapa Flow early on the 24th. His whole fleet was busy refuelling when he received news of the Easter Rebellion in Dublin, with a warning that some sympathetic German action was to be expected: Scheer had arranged a bombardment of Lowestoft as bait to draw British units into the maw of the German Battle Fleet which left its base early on 24th April. That afternoon the *Seydlitz* was seriously damaged by a British mine and had to return to harbour. Rear-Admiral Bödicker, who was temporarily in command of the Scouting Groups whilst Hipper was ill, transferred his flag to the *Lützow* and by nightfall had resumed his position 50 miles ahead of Scheer. But long before this Room 40 gleaned enough from the Germans' prodigal use of radio to warn Jellicoe that the High Seas Fleet was out; by 1950 the Admiralty had sufficient information to order the Grand Fleet south to intercept.

Since Beatty was without two of his ships, Jellicoe sent his fast Fifth Battle Squadron (the 'Queen Elizabeth' class) on ahead to augment the Battlecruiser Fleet. The Harwich Force and 12 submarines were also ordered to positions which the Admiralty believed would be suitable for intercepting the enemy. With a fine disregard for instructions he judged to be wrong, Tyrwhitt took his ships towards Lowestoft. He was rewarded at first light (0350) on the 25th by sighting the four German battlecruisers to the northward. Lacking the force to make a direct attack, he manœuvred his ships in the hope of enticing the enemy in pursuit. But Bödicker was too close to his objective to be deflected from it; at 0410 his squadron began a ten-minute bombardment of Lowestoft. Having destroyed 200 houses he swung north to attack Yarmouth, but no sooner had his heavy ships opened fire than his cruisers reported being in action with Tyrwhitt's ships, and he decided to go to their support. Yarmouth was thus saved at the cost of a brief action in which one hit was scored on the light cruiser *Conquest*. For though Bödicker had it in his power to destroy his spirited but puny opponent, he chose to retire eastwards towards Scheer's Battle Fleet which had already (0520) reversed course for home. Tyrwhitt followed until 0845 when the Admiralty ordered him to return to harbour, whilst the Battlecruiser Fleet, coming south at full speed, missed

Bödicker by only 45 miles before Beatty, too, reversed course for home.

The Grand Fleet attempted a retaliatory operation on 3rd May when Jellicoe sailed two forces, one with orders to lay mines off the end of the German swept channels, the other to make a second air attack on the Tondern sheds. They were supported by the Battle Fleet and by Beatty's battlecruisers in the expectation that these activities on the Germans' doorstep would draw the High Seas Fleet from its lair. But the minelaying went undetected and all except one of the attacking planes were unable to take off in the prevailing swell. Scheer, who was distracted by the need to succour eight of his zeppelins which chanced to be returning from a raid on Britain, did not realize that British forces were out until late on 4th May; by the time he sailed Jellicoe had ordered his ships home.

The German Chancellor cited the Lowestoft raid as evidence that Britain no longer held command of the sea in order to compel an indefinite postponement of a new U-boat campaign. In Britain 'the impunity with which the enemy had insulted our east coast after his long inactivity came with something of a shock to public opinion' (*Corbett*); Balfour promised the Mayors of Lowestoft and Yarmouth a redeployment of the Fleet designed to prevent it happening again. This had been under discussion for the past year for more reasons than the need for a sufficient force to be based where it could best intercept an enemy sortie against the English coast. Six months earlier Beatty, who had shown his interest in gunnery before the war by successfully pressing the Admiralty to allow his battlecruisers to carry out full calibre practices at the realistic speed of 20 knots instead of the regulation ten, had expressed concern at the effects of the lack of practice facilities secure from submarine attack at Rosyth: 'We must keep our gunnery up; our opportunities here are nil,' he wrote. Jellicoe's suggested solution was for the battlecruisers to go in turn to Scapa where such facilities were available in the Flow, but even when he criticized the poor results of practices carried out by the battlecruisers in October, Beatty maintained that none could be spared to go north. Early in 1916, he proposed that his Battlecruiser Fleet should be strengthened by exchanging the well-armoured Fifth Battle Squadron for the three lightly armoured 'Invincibles'. Jellicoe would not, however, accept the argument that there was no disparity in speed; he maintained that the 'Queen Elizabeths' were only good for 23½ knots, compared with the 'Invincibles' 25, and were, therefore, too slow for Beatty's purpose. Finally, in February 1916, the War Committee, after again rejecting Fisher's concept of an amphibious landing in the Baltic, had urged Jellicoe to bring his whole Battle Fleet south to Rosyth. Quoting his letter of 30th October 1914, as well as mentioning the inadequacy of the anti-submarine defences of the Firth of Forth for a force far too large to lie above the Bridge, the Commander-in-Chief refused: 'the safety and overwhelming strength of the Grand Fleet was Jellicoe's all-embracing aim; it had become ingrained in his nature' (*Churchill*). The Committee proposed the alternative of adding the Fifth Battle Squadron to Beatty's command, Bradford's pre-dreadnoughts being moved to the Humber or Thames. This, too, Jellicoe opposed on the score that the 'Queen Elizabeths' were needed as a fast wing for his battle fleet. But the Lowestoft raid compelled action; the Third Battle Squadron arrived off Sheerness at the beginning of May, and a conference held at Rosyth on the 12th decided that the defences of the Firth of Forth should be hastened to completion so that Jellicoe's Battle Fleet could be moved there. In the interval, either the Fifth or the Fourth Battle Squadron would be sent to Rosyth from time to time, whilst the battlecruiser squadrons would go to Scapa in turn for gunnery practices. But this decision was taken too late to do much more than improve the gunnery efficiency of one of Beatty's squadrons before the next crucial sortie by the High Seas Fleet.

So we come to the middle of May 1916 and the operations with which four months of lunge and counter-lunge by the British and German fleets culminated in a major battle. This chapter has marked the different maritime strategies of the two nations, the personalities and qualities of their principal naval leaders and some of the merits and shortcomings of their ships and methods. Another factor remains to be mentioned. To the British Fleet the gun was the decisive weapon, as it had been for the past 400 years—and Jellicoe was a gunnery specialist. The over-riding purpose of his cruisers and battlecruisers was to enable his battle fleet to gain contact with the enemy. The first duty of his destroyers was to protect it from torpedo attacks; such attacks on the enemy were a secondary duty.* The core of Jellicoe's concept of a battle was a gunnery duel between ships-of-the-line on similar courses,

* To be more exact Jellicoe had recently decided to reverse these priorities; but the necessary instructions to the Fleet had not been issued by the time Jutland was fought.

albeit at a greater range than in previous wars and subject to the need to avoid torpedo fire, which meant 15,000 yards, decreasing to 10,000 when the enemy had been dominated. Except that the Fifth Battle Squadron would be stationed, preferably in the van, otherwise in the rear, from where its margin of four knots might enable it to turn the enemy line, there was little in the *Grand Fleet Battle Orders* embodying 'the whole art of tactics, massing superior forces against part of the opposing fleet'. (*Dewar*)

The recently created German Navy, unhampered by centuries of tradition, believed that the torpedo could be as decisive as the gun—and Scheer was a torpedo specialist. His cruisers and battlecruisers had a twofold task, to enable his Battle Fleet to gain contact with a part of the Grand Fleet but to avoid the whole of it. His torpedoboats' prime duty was to execute a massed torpedo attack; beating off enemy destroyers was their secondary duty. His battleships would fight a gunnery duel if they encountered a weaker enemy force; if they met one as strong, or stronger, they would retire rapidly out of range under cover of smoke.

These different tactical concepts of a day action were, of course, incompatible—and it will be noted that Scheer's did not include submarines and minelayers operating with the High Seas Fleet as Jellicoe expected, for which reason the latter did not envisage pursuit of a fleeing enemy. The British Admiral was unlikely to score a decisive victory unless he managed to manœuvre his opponent into a position from which he could not evade the heavier broadsides of the Grand Fleet. He depended, moreover, on good visibility. Conversely, poor visibility would favour Scheer's method which was limited to inflicting damage on a single battle squadron or a similar inferior British force. Unless these considerable differences, which stemmed from the likewise incompatible strategic aims of the two navies, are borne in mind, it is easy to misjudge the achievements of the rival Commanders-in-Chief when the fickle fortunes of war allowed their fleets to meet off the coast of Jutland on 31st May 1916.

3

'Der Tag'

'We were haunted by the fear that possibly "the day" may never come.'

Admiral Beatty to King George V

'On the afternoon of Wednesday 31st May a naval engagement took place off the coast of Jutland. The British ships on which the brunt of the fighting fell were the Battlecruiser Fleet supported by four fast battleships.'

Admiralty communiqué of 2nd June 1916

HAVING SUCCESSFULLY trodden on John Bull's corns, Scheer decided to aim a kick at his shins. By bombarding Lowestoft he had, in his own words, 'forced the enemy to send out his forces', but the result had been no more than a brush with Tyrwhitt's ships; the High Seas Fleet had crossed the North Sea too far to the south to trap any part of the Grand Fleet. A more northerly port, Sunderland, was therefore chosen as the next target for Hipper's battlecruisers. Since this involved a greater risk of meeting the British Battle Fleet, Scheer postulated two conditions: the High Seas Fleet would only sail after its zeppelins had carried out a reconnaissance to ensure that Jellicoe was not already at sea; and a number of U-boats, which were now limited to 'purely military enterprises', would be sent to lay mines off the Grand Fleet's harbours and to attack any units which might put to sea.

This bombardment was set for 17th May, 17 U-boats being sailed so that ten would be off Scapa Flow, Cromarty and the Forth, and the rest in other positions by that date. Too late to recall them, Scheer learned that the *Seydlitz*'s repairs would not be completed in time; moreover seven ships of his Third Battle Squadron developed 'condenseritis'. The operation was postponed to the 23rd. At 0200 on the previous morning *U47*, to seaward of Sunderland, reported everything clear for the attack, but the same day brought news that the *Seydlitz*'s repairs were unsatisfactory. Unwilling to proceed without one of his five battlecruisers, Scheer again postponed the operation, to 29th May. Since this was dangerously near to 1st June, the last day on which the U-boats could remain on patrol, the German Commander-in-Chief devised an alternative plan. If adverse weather prevented the zeppelin reconnaissance required for the bombardment, the High Seas Fleet would entice British units out by showing itself off the south-west coast of Norway. (Scheer did not, of course, know that the High Seas Fleet could disclose its position at any time by the use of wireless to the British direction-finding stations.)

Scheer's submarines had not found their tasks easy. British patrols destroyed *U74*, one of three minelaying boats. Another developed leaky tanks and had to return to port with her mines unlaid. *U75* laid her field to the north-west of the Orkneys where it had no effect on Jutland but, by a tragic quirk of fate, sank the cruiser *Hampshire* carrying Kitchener to Russia on 5th June. *UB27* actually entered the Firth of Forth but fouled nets off Inchkeith. After lying on the bottom for 24 hours, her captain could only clear one propeller. This obliged him to abandon an intended attack on the Battlecruiser Fleet at anchor and to return to Germany on one engine. Such vicissitudes resulted in only four U-boats being still in positions where they could sight units of the Grand Fleet leaving harbour on 30th May, when adverse winds prevented zeppelins taking the air, which decided Scheer to execute his alternative plan.

On 31st May the First Scouting Group of five battlecruisers, with Hipper's flag in the *Lützow*, left the Jade at 0200, accompanied by the Second Scouting Group of four light cruisers under Rear-Admiral Bödicker in the *Frankfurt* and the Second, Sixth and Ninth Flotillas, comprising 30 torpedoboats led by Commodore Heinrich in the light cruiser *Regensburg*. 'The absence of air reconnaissance [having] made it essential to keep all forces concentrated as much as possible', Rear-Admiral Behncke in the *König* headed six other dreadnoughts of the Third Battle Squadron past the Jade lightship at 0230. Scheer followed in the *Friedrich der Grosse*, leading Vice-Admiral Schmidt in the *Ostfriesland* and seven more dreadnoughts of the First Battle Squadron, plus Rear-Admiral Mauve in the *Deutschland* and five more pre-dreadnoughts of the Second Battle Squadron. Although these last ships, with their slow speed and limited gunpower, could be of no real assistance if Scheer succeeded in his purpose, and must delay his retirement if he ran into Jellicoe's Battle Fleet, they were included for the human, but not otherwise justifiable, reasons of sentiment for Scheer's old command, and because Mauve protested strongly against being left behind. These three battle squadrons were accompanied by the Fourth Scouting Group of five light cruisers under Commodore Reuter in the *Stettin* and by Commodore Michelson in the light cruiser *Rostock*, leading the First Third, Fifth and Seventh Flotillas, totalling 31 torpedoboats.* By 0800 Scheer's Battle Fleet, following 50 miles astern of Hipper's force, had cleared Heligoland and was heading north up the swept channel through' the minefields towards the Horn Reefs lightvessel in fine weather marred only by a force 3 north-westerly wind† which prevented his fragile zeppelins leaving their sheds.

In the third week of May Rear-Admiral Hood's Third Battlecruiser Squadron had gone north to Scapa to carry out gunnery practices while as agreed at the conference held on the 12th, Rear-Admiral Evan-Thomas's Fifth Battle Squadron came south to Rosyth. That this might have repercussions on the Grand Fleet's tactics, if it should be ordered to sea to counter an enemy sortie, was understood by Jellicoe and Beatty. Hood's ships were no substitute for Evan-Thomas's: they could only be used as a spearhead for Jellicoe's cruisers. The British battle fleet would, therefore, be without the fast van squadron with which the Commander-in-Chief envisaged achieving a concentration of fire on part of the enemy line. On the other hand, if the heavy guns and armour of the Fifth Battle Squadron were to be an adjunct to the Battlecruiser Fleet, Beatty would have to allow for its slightly slower speed. For these reasons neither Admiral issued any instructions for using the temporarily attached squadrons with their own fleets; Beatty intended that, at the first opportunity, Evan-Thomas should rejoin Jellicoe, whom he knew would send Hood to the Battlecruiser Fleet.

During the latter part of May Jellicoe was planning an operation with much the same object as Scheer's: two light cruiser squadrons would sweep into the Kattegat on 2nd June; in the hope that this would entice the High Seas Fleet out, they were to be supported by the rest of the Grand Fleet. Before this could happen the Admiralty noted the number of U-boats in the North Sea that were not attacking shipping,

* For further details of the High Seas Fleet see Appendix II.
† Later in the day it backed to SW.

which suggested some unusual enemy move. Room 40 confirmed this early on 30th May by deciphering Scheer's signal warning them that 'Hostile forces may proceed to sea',* followed by one ordering the High Seas Fleet to be assembled in the Outer Jade by 1900. The Harwich Force was recalled to harbour and a preliminary warning sent to Jellicoe at noon. A little later the Third Battle Squadron in the Thames Estuary was ordered to have steam by daylight next morning. In the course of the afternoon Room 40 supplied enough intelligence for the Admiralty to signal Jellicoe and Beatty at 1740: 'Germans intend some operations commencing tomorrow leaving via Horn Reefs. You should concentrate to eastward of Long Forties [an area 60 miles east of the Scottish coast] ready for eventualities.' So the Battle Fleet was ordered to prepare to leave Scapa and Cromarty, whilst at Rosyth the *Lion* flew the signal, 'Raise steam for 22 knots and report when ready to proceed'. A quarter of an hour later Jellicoe heard that the Harwich Force and Third Battle Squadron would not be ordered out until more was known; but Tyrwhitt was instructed to have steam at one hour's notice by daylight on the 31st. Beatty received his instructions from Jellicoe at 2015; the Battlecruiser Fleet was to steer for a position 100 miles NW of the Horn Reefs Light (57°45'N, 4°15'E), arriving there at 1400 on the 31st, at which time Jellicoe's Battle Fleet would reach a position 65 miles to the northward. If there was no news by 1400 Beatty was to turn north towards Jellicoe, who would steer south for the Horn Reefs.

At 2130 the *Lion* led the battlecruisers to sea, the three ships of the First Battlecruiser Squadron under Rear-Admiral Brock in the *Princess Royal* being followed by two of the Second under Rear-Admiral Pakenham in the *New Zealand*.

> The battlecruisers slipped their moorings and began to feel their way towards the unseen entrance of the harbour. From the bridge of each mass of towering shadows the stern light of the next ahead could be discerned dimly through binoculars, and on these pin-points they steered. What the flagship steered by, in the narrow confines of the crowded harbour and inky blackness, only the little knot of figures on her forebridge knew, the Admiral and Flag Captain, the Navigator and Officer-of-the-Watch moving mysteriously about the glow-worm arc of light from the binnacle and chart-table. One by one the long black shapes slid through the outer defences, ebon shadows in a world of

* To the Admiralty this was made to appear more threatening by a deciphering error; Room 40's version read: '*German* forces may proceed to sea'.

shades. The escorting destroyers came pelting up astern, heralded by the rush and rattle of spray-thrashed steel, funnels glowing and the roar of their fans from the engine-room exhausts. Night and the mystery of darkness enfolded them. The battlecruisers were unleashed. (*'Bartimeus'*)

They were accompanied by four ships of the Fifth Battle Squadron with Evan-Thomas's flag in the *Barham*; by the First, Second and Third Light Cruiser Squadrons, each of the four ships, commanded respectively by Commodore Alexander-Sinclair in the *Galatea*, Commodore Good-enough in the *Southampton* and Rear-Admiral Napier in the *Falmouth*; by the First, Ninth, Tenth and Thirteenth Flotillas, totalling two light cruisers and 27 destroyers; and by the small seaplane-carrier *Engadine*. At the same hour the Battle Fleet left Scapa Flow and Cromarty, 24 dreadnoughts, including Jellicoe's flagship, the *Iron Duke*, divided into the First Battle Squadron commanded by Vice-Admiral Burney in the *Marlborough*, the Second by Vice-Admiral Jerram in the *King George V* and the Fourth by Vice-Admiral Sturdee, victor of the Falklands, in the *Benbow*. With them went the Third Battlecruiser Squadron led by Hood in the *Invincible*; the First and Second Cruiser Squadrons, each of four armoured cruisers, the one commanded by Rear-Admiral Arbuthnot in the *Defence*, the other by Rear-Admiral Heath in the *Minotaur*; Commodore Le Mesurier's Fourth Light Cruiser Squadron of five ships led by the *Calliope*; seven other light cruisers; the Fourth, Eleventh and Twelfth Flotillas totalling 50 destroyers; and the mine-layer *Abdiel**—all 'moving south in support, ringed by the misty horizon of the North Sea, with the calling gulls following the white furrows of their keels like crows after the plough' (*'Bartimeus'*). The large seaplane-carrier *Campania* should have accompanied them but was held back by an engine defect. With this exception the Grand Fleet, thanks to Room 40, had sailed four-and-a-half hours *before* the first units of the High Seas Fleet left the Jade.†

Early next morning *U32*, patrolling to seaward of the Firth of Forth, sighted the Battlecruiser Fleet, fired two torpedoes which missed the *Galatea*, and was nearly rammed by the *Phaeton*. From Lieutenant von Peckelsheim Scheer received a report at 0530 of two dreadnoughts, two cruisers and several destroyers steering a south-easterly course. An hour later Lieutenant von Bothmer of *U66*, who failed to attack Jerram's

---

* Which could lay 72 mines. Contrary to Jellicoe's expectations, no German ship at Jutland carried them.

† For further details of the Grand Fleet see Appendix I.

squadron on its way out of Cromarty, reported eight enemy dreadnoughts, with light cruisers and destroyers steering a north-easterly course. These contradictory messages told the German Commander-in-Chief nothing which he could interpret as affecting his own operation, so he held his northerly course. There can therefore be only one assessment of his plan to use U-boats: notwithstanding their number they neither provided him with useful intelligence nor reduced the strength of the Grand Fleet which was now heading towards him in the overwhelming strength which from the outset had been Jellicoe's aim:

	Grand Fleet	High Seas Fleet
Battleships : dreadnoughts	28[1]	16[3] } 22
pre-dreadnoughts	—	6[4]
Battlecruisers	9[2]	5[5]
Armoured cruisers	8	—
Light cruisers	26	11
Destroyers/Torpedoboats	77	61
Seaplane-carrier	1	—
Minelayer	1	—

Notes

[1] All Britain's dreadnoughts except for the *Emperor of India* and *Queen Elizabeth* which were refitting, the *Royal Sovereign* which had been too recently commissioned to be an effective fighting unit, and the *Dreadnought* herself which was flagship of the Third Battle Squadron.

[2] All Britain's battlecruisers except the *Australia* which was in dockyard hands.

[3] All Germany's dreadnoughts except for the *König Albert* which was refitting, and the too recently commissioned *Bayern*.

[4] The *Preussen* and *Lothringen* were absent, the former having been detached for duty in the Baltic, the latter being unfit for service.

[5] All Germany's battlecruisers except the *Goeben*.

In gun power the British also had a considerable preponderance of strength*:

Battle Fleet	British	German
11-inch	—	72 }
12-inch	128[1]	128
13·5-inch	110 } 264	— } 200
14-inch	10	—
15-inch	16	—

* A small increase in calibre allowed a large increase in projectile weight:

Calibre	Projectile weight
11-inch	665 lb.
12-inch	890 lb.
13·5-inch	1250/1400 lb.
15-inch	1920 lb.

Battlecruiser Fleet/Scouting Groups	British	German
11-inch	—	28 ⎫
12-inch	16 ⎫	16 ⎪ 44
13·5-inch	32 ⎬ 80	— ⎬
15-inch	32² ⎭	— ⎭

Notes

¹ Includes the Third Battlecruiser Squadron.
² Those of the Fifth Battle Squadron.

The Grand Fleet had other advantages: four of Beatty's battlecruisers could steam three knots faster than any of Hipper's; the best speed of Jellicoe's battle fleet was one knot faster than Scheer's—four knots faster if the German Commander-in-Chief kept Mauve's pre-dreadnoughts in company; Beatty had the Fifth Battle Squadron whose ships were as fast as the *Moltke* and *Von der Tann* and more heavily armed than any German vessel; and the Germans were so short of cruisers that they were obliged to augment their look-out screens with torpedoboats. Indeed, Scheer's force only matched Jellicoe's in one respect; it was armed with as many torpedo tubes. (British 382 21-inch and 75 18-inch: German 362 19·7-inch and 107 17·7-inch.)

In a sentence, Jellicoe had a fleet double the size of Scheer's, able to fire more than twice the weight of shell. Moreover, in addition to the six completed dreadnought battleships and battlecruisers which were absent from the Grand Fleet, seven more heavy ships armed with 15-inch guns were on the stocks, against which Scheer's only reserves were two ships recently completed and two building. Surely then, and in sharp contrast to the first year of the war, the British Commander-in-Chief, notwithstanding intelligence reports which suggested that the High Seas Fleet had been augmented by two more dreadnoughts, and that most of its battleships had been rearmed with bigger guns, would be justified in accepting the possible loss of some of his dreadnoughts in order to maul, if not destroy, his opponent. As surely, if Scheer should fail to avoid so great a force, he must suffer a decisive defeat. Before the sun went down, 31st May 1916 could have the same memorable place in British history as 21st October 1805.

At 0500 Jellicoe's Battle Fleet altered course to S50E and steamed at 16 knots, reducing to 14 at noon, towards the rendezvous for which Beatty's battlecruisers were heading east at 19. But Tyrwhitt, after reminding the Admiralty that his force was still awaiting orders, was told to remain in Harwich harbour at one hour's notice. This decision appeared to be justified at 1235 when the Admiralty signalled: 'No definite news of enemy. It was thought fleet had sailed but directional signal places flagship in Jade at 1110. Apparently they have been unable to carry out air reconnaissance which has delayed them.'

> The Room 40 staff were still, in the eyes of the Operations staff, a party of very clever fellows who could decipher signals, [but] any suggestion that they should interpret them would have been resented. On the morning of 31st May an officer of the Operations Division [Rear-Admiral Thomas Jackson,* Director of Operations, who had a profound distrust of Room 40's activities] entered and asked where directionals placed call-sign DK. On being told 'in the Jade', he went out without asking questions. If he had discussed the situation with the officer-in-charge he would have learnt that DK was the German C.-in-C.'s *harbour* call-sign and that when he went to sea he transferred [it] to a harbour station and used another one. (*Admiral Sir William James*)

As a result of this lack of co-operation the Admiralty sent a signal which to Jellicoe and Beatty could only mean that, if any part of the High Seas Fleet was out, it did not include Scheer's battle fleet. (Room 40 had been unable to decipher the following signal from Scheer to the High Seas Fleet which would have prevented this mistake and advised Jellicoe to arrive earlier in the battle area: 'The head of the Third Battle Squadron will pass Jade war lightship at 0330. Second Squadron will take part in the operation and will join up astern of First Squadron. Wilhelmshaven Third Entrance will control W/T [wireless] in German Bight'.) Jellicoe had, therefore, no reason to amend his orders to Beatty to turn north at 1400 when 65 miles should have separated the two British forces. He had adopted this considerable distance, instead of a tactically more desirable one of about 40 miles, so that his Battle Fleet was where it could cover the Tenth Cruiser Squadron which enforced the North Sea blockade between the Shetlands and Norway, whilst his Battlecruiser Fleet was far enough to the south to deal with another German raid on the east coast, which seemed their likely intention from the intelligence available.

In preparation for the alteration Beatty stationed the Second Battle-cruiser Squadron three miles ENE of the First, and moved the Fifth

* Not to be confused with Admiral Sir Henry Jackson, First Sea Lord.

8 *British battlecruisers in the North Sea:* (*l. to r.*) Queen Mary, Princess Royal, Lion

9 *The first aircraft carrier to take part in a major naval action:* H.M.S. Engadine

10 *A typical British destroyer of the First World War*

11 *Flagship of the Second Light Cruiser Squadron:* H.M.S. Southampton

Battle Squadron on to a bearing NNW from the *Lion*, distant five miles, ready to take its place in the van of Jellicoe's battle fleet. But, having been delayed for half an hour during the morning by the need to examine suspicious trawlers, he held his easterly course until 1415 before signalling his force to swing round to NbyE. Alexander-Sinclair's, Napier's and Goodenough's cruisers were then spread on a look-out line running ENE-WSW, eight miles SSE from the *Lion*.

> The *Galatea* was just about to turn [recalls one of her officers] when a merchant ship was sighted [to the east] blowing off steam, so the Commodore [Alexander-Sinclair] held on to have a look at her. A destroyer was observed to leave her side and by her stump foremast and tall mainmast to be a Hun. Action stations were at once sounded off. As I went up the ladder on to the forecastle I was deafened by the report of the 6-inch gun firing and was almost blown down again by the blast. I nipped into my little [coding office] quicker than it takes to tell and as I entered there rattled down the tube from the bridge the first enemy report.

Since the German Commander-in-Chief had received no news to suggest that he might encounter a British force, the High Seas Fleet was still on its course for Norway, with Hipper's battlecruisers 60 miles to the north of Scheer's battleships. Thus, all unknown to both Hipper and Beatty, only 50 miles separated their battlecruisers at 1400. Moreover, Beatty's alteration towards Jellicoe brought him on to a similar course to Hipper with the wings of their respective look-out screens separated by only 22 miles. They might, nonetheless, have remained out of sight of each other but for the chance presence of the Danish steamer *N.J. Fjord* midway between them. Captain Madlung of the light cruiser *Elbing*, on the western wing of Hipper's screen, sent two torpedoboats to board this innocent vessel which was sighted soon afterwards by the *Galatea* on the eastern wing of Beatty's screen. The contact was reported by Alexander-Sinclair soon after 1420 as 'two cruisers probably hostile in sight bearing ESE'.* Madlung wirelessed a similar signal to Scheer and Hipper as the *Elbing*'s guns answered the *Galatea*'s at 1428 and drew first blood at a range of 15,000 yards although, ironically enough in the light of later events, this first German shell to hit a British ship failed to explode. So the Battle of Jutland

---

* This and most similar signals included the reporting ship's position, whence it was possible for recipients to plot the position of the enemy, but there is no point in reproducing these positions here.

began with neither side knowing that the other's main fleet was anywhere near the scene, Scheer because his zeppelins had been unable to take the air, Jellicoe for the less excusable reason that the Admiralty had misinterpreted the intelligence in their possession.

A note of caution must be sounded before unfolding how the action developed out of this chance contact. The difference between the *Victory* and a twentieth-century battleship is too great for a student of Trafalgar to misjudge Nelson's or Villeneuve's tactics. But the 'Queen Elizabeth' class, of which four comprised the Fifth Battle Squadron at Jutland, also played a notable part in the Second World War. There were, however, important technical innovations in the intervening quarter of a century which were not available to Jellicoe or Scheer. Neither side had aircraft, apart from Germany's unreliable zeppelins and the few seaplanes in the *Engadine*. Ships were fitted with wireless telegraphy, but the message capacity of spark transmitters and crystal detector receivers was extremely limited. So as to enable signals to be passed by flags or searchlight between units of a force so large as the Grand Fleet, Jellicoe was obliged to employ light cruisers whose main task was to repeat signals hoisted by his flagship. Others had to be stationed as signal links between the *Iron Duke* and his armoured cruisers spread as scouts ahead of the battle fleet.

Such measures did not, however, do much towards easing the chief handicap which both fleets suffered: the area of sea which each covered, and the increase in gun range since Tsushima, was such that neither Admiral could direct the battle by what he could see from his flagship's bridge, as Togo had done only ten years before; both depended on reports signalled by their ships, especially their cruiser forces. But the methods available for plotting these reports were inadequate for providing a comprehensive picture, which was further confused by discrepancies in positions, many ships being fitted with nothing better than a magnetic compass.* At Jutland a natural hazard increased these handicaps, especially since radar had yet to be conceived. Though the weather was fine apart from low cloud, the slight mist which limited visibility to eight miles at the outset of the action thickened as the day wore on, funnel smoke from many ships steaming at high speed and the brown cordite fumes of gunfire combining to reduce it to

---

* For which reason all courses and bearings in contemporary signals and reports were magnetic, a custom followed in this book. The variation was only 13°W.

four miles or less. No admiral or captain could then see more than a few of his own ships and even fewer of the enemy's; often he had only a fleeting glimpse of a target which disappeared as soon as his guns had fired half-a-dozen salvoes. In effect, the British and German Fleets were compelled to fight much of Jutland as if blindfold, a disadvantage which neither Nelson nor Togo suffered when they annihilated their enemies and one which is all too easily overlooked when judging the battle.

The inherent inaccuracy of long-range naval gunfire at the time of Jutland must also be remembered. In peace-time practices dreadnoughts had achieved results comparable with those of ships-of-the-line fighting at point-blank range: 70 per cent of hits with 12-inch guns firing at a target towed at eight knots on a predetermined parallel course at a range of 8,000 yards. But in war with ships steaming at 20 knots or more, with the course of the enemy unknown and frequently changing, and ranges of 12,000 yards or greater, five per cent of hits was as good as could be expected, whilst if the battle took the form of a chase, as at the Falklands, it was less than this. A prolonged gunnery duel, involving the expenditure of the greater part of ships' outfits of ammunition,* might therefore be necessary to achieve a decisive result unless one or other side chanced to obtain disabling hits early in the action, as on the *Blücher* and the *Lion* at the Dogger Bank.

British battleships and battlecruisers had the better fire-control equipment: whereas the Germans had no more than an instrument for transmitting the bearing of the target, a range clock and a simple device for calculating the enemy's rate and deflection,† the British ships (except the *Erin* and *Agincourt*) were fitted with Admiral Sir Percy Scott's director whereby all their big guns were aimed and fired from a single sight mounted aloft, clear of smoke and spray, and with Captain F. C. Dreyer's fire-control table. The German vessels were, however, fitted with stereoscopic rangefinders which were more accurate than the British coincidence type. So, whilst the British were better equipped to 'hold' their targets once the range had been found, which suited Jellicoe's tactical concept of a prolonged gunnery duel, the

* Dreadnoughts carried 100 rounds per gun for their main armament whose best rate of fire was two rounds per gun per minute.

† Rate of change of range and deflection enable a gun's sights to be set so as to allow for the movement of the target during the time of flight of a shell—about half a minute at 12,000 yards, in which a 25-knot ship can travel nearly a quarter of a mile.

Germans were more likely to score hits with their initial salvoes, as Spee had done at Coronel, which matched Scheer's intention of avoiding action with a superior fleet.

Beatty's reaction to the *Galatea*'s initial enemy report was characteristically quick. Although he could count on the other three ships of the First Light Cruiser Squadron hurrying to their Commodore's support, 'two cruisers, probably hostile' suggested that a larger German force might not be far away. Telling Chatfield, his Flag Captain, to put the *Lion*'s helm over without waiting for the signal to be answered— the usual practice when it was desired to save time—he ordered his ships to swing back to SSE. The First Battlecruiser Squadron followed the *Lion* round; the Second also turned; but the *Barham* was too far away for her signal staff to read the *Lion*'s flags. Evan-Thomas, his attention diverted by the *Galatea*'s report from looking to the northward for Jellicoe's Battle Fleet, saw the battlecruisers turning. His Flag Captain, Craig, urged him to conform but the Admiral had been schooled to obey orders; he waited seven minutes for the *Lion* to pass the new course by searchlight.* Before this the *Barham* had altered on to the port leg of a routine zigzag which turned her squadron even further from SSE than NbyE; moreover, at 1432 Beatty increased speed to 22 knots. By the time the Fifth Battle Squadron came round the distance separating the *Barham* from the *Lion* was not five miles but ten—and ten miles astern at that, which was the more significant since the battleships had no margin of speed over the battlecruisers. Beatty's impetuous decision, borne of his experience of the enemy's congenital desire to avoid action, coupled with the delay in passing his signal to the *Barham* and Evan-Thomas's refusal to act without it, thus combined to deprive the battlecruisers of the immediate support of four battleships. In 1927 Evan-Thomas explained his failure in these words:

> The only way I could account for no signal having been received by me was that the Vice-Admiral [Beatty] was going to signal another course to the Fifth Battle Squadron, possibly to get the enemy light cruisers between us. Anyway, if he wished us to turn, the searchlight would have done it in a moment. It was not until the *Tiger* asked the *Lion* by

* At 0428 the *Tiger*, rear ship of the First Battlecruiser Squadron, had been made responsible for repeating Beatty's signals to the *Barham*, then stationed on her quarter. The *Lion*'s signal staff overlooked the *Tiger*'s inability to do this after an alteration of course which placed the *Barham* on the *Lion*'s bow until the *Tiger* queried whether the *Lion* had assumed this responsibility.

wireless whether the signal to turn was to be made to the *Barham* that the Vice-Admiral seemed to realize the situation.

Beatty's 'failure' (as Jellicoe subsequently characterized it) to concentrate his force at this stage was to have more serious repercussions than a mistake made by the German battlecruisers. Bödicker's light cruisers turned west and steamed at full speed to the *Elbing*'s support; not so Hipper. Initially uncertain of the identity of the torpedoboats alongside the N.J. Fjord, the *Galatea* challenged them with the current British recognition signal. Recognizing its potential value, the *Elbing* passed this to the *Lützow* where it was misread as a sighting report of 24–26 battleships! Hipper promptly turned his battlecruisers away to SSW. It did not, however, take the German Admiral long to elucidate the inaccuracy of this unlikely signal; at 1452 he turned back to WNW to support Bödicker's squadron and at 1500, five minutes after the latter had identified his opponents as four light cruisers, increased speed to 23 knots in the hope of cutting them off.

At 1440 Alexander-Sinclair, in pursuit of the *Elbing*, had signalled: 'Have sighted large amount of smoke as though from a fleet bearing ENE'. Ten minutes later he confirmed Beatty's belief that such an apparently portentous message was no more than normal signal book phraseology by adding, 'Smoke seems to be seven vessels besides destroyers and cruisers. They have turned north'. This made it clear 'that the enemy was to the north and east and that it would be impossible for him to round the Horn Reefs without being brought to action'. Nonetheless, Beatty was so determined to do this that he continued to lead his battlecruisers at their maximum available speed towards the 'sound of the guns', notwithstanding the distance by which the Fifth Battle Squadron lagged behind.

At 1447 Beatty ordered the *Engadine* to send up one of her Short seaplanes to reconnoitre. Lieutenant-Commander Robinson's crew beat their best time for opening the unwieldy hangar doors, drawing a 'sticks and string' machine out on to the deck, spreading its wings, running up its 225-h.p. engine and hoisting it into the sea. Yet, it was 21 minutes before Flight Lieutenant Rutland and his observer, Assistant-Paymaster Trewin, were airborne, cloud forcing them to fly at 1,000 ft. Ten minutes later they sighted the enemy.

To tell what they were I had to close to within a mile and a half. They then opened fire on me with anti-aircraft and other guns. The shock of exploding shrapnel could be felt, the explosions taking place about 200 ft. away. When [Trewin] had counted and got the disposition of the enemy and was making his report, I steered to about three miles, keeping the enemy well in sight, and as the weather cleared a little I observed the disposition of our fleet. The picture from the air of the battlecruisers and of the 'Queen Elizabeth' class battleships, with their attendant light cruiser screen and destroyers, all rushing forward to cut off the enemy is [one] that can never be forgotten. At 1545 a petrol pipe leading to the left carburettor broke, my engine revolutions dropped and I was forced to descend. On landing I made good the defect with rubber tube and reported that I could go on again [but] I was told to come alongside and be hoisted in.

Since this was the first instance of a heavier-than-air machine being used in a fleet action, one must regret that Rutland and Trewin's work should have been in vain; their wireless reports reached the *Engadine* but she was unable to pass them to the *Lion*. Nor were her planes used again during Jutland; the prevailing swell, though slight, made it impracticable for such fragile machines, with their canvas and plywood floats, to take off.* Beatty had to depend on the reports signalled by Alexander-Sinclair as the First Light Cruiser Squadron deliberately drew the enemy to the NW, whilst the British battlecruisers turned to E at 1500, and to NE increasing speed to 23 knots at 1513, to cut the enemy off from their base—when Evan-Thomas, by taking short cuts, was able to reduce the distance by which his squadron lagged to some six miles on Beatty's port quarter. 'There was now an excellent opportunity for Beatty [to concentrate] his forces. The enemy was steering towards our Battle Fleet so that the loss of two or three miles on the part of the battlecruisers was immaterial. But the opportunity was not taken' (*Jellicoe*). The signal 'BJ One' had already gone to the flagship's masthead: 'Assume complete readiness for action'. It had been answered by that most stirring of sights, battle ensigns hoisted to the yard arms of the *Princess Royal*, *Queen Mary*, *Tiger*, *New Zealand* and *Indefatigable* as, in that order, they followed Beatty in the *Lion*.

Action stations followed by the bugle 'double' were sounded off [recalls an officer in the *Princess Royal*]. All communications, instruments,

---

* Which should be a sufficient answer to those who criticize Jellicoe for not allowing the *Campania* to leave Scapa because she failed to receive the sailing signal in time. She could have caught up the British battle fleet by 1330 so that her ten planes would have been at Jellicoe's disposal when he needed their reports; but it is unlikely that they could have taken off. Moreover, even if they had done so, would their reports have fared any better than Rutland's?

etc. were quickly tested. The various [fire and repair] parties were mustered at their stations; gasmasks, goggles and life-saving belts produced and all other final preparations for action made. Splinter mats, fire hoses, boxes of sand, stretchers, medical instruments and drugs, leak-stopping gear, shoring-up spars, spare electrical gear, spare hydraulic gear, engineers spare gear—all these and the various other action accessories were ready in a few minutes.

In as short a time turret crews manned gunhouses, magazines and shellrooms and, with no more fuss than they had shown at drill, responded to the order: 'Load! Load! Load!'—whilst on the bridge of the *New Zealand* Captain Green donned his *piu-piu*, the Maori garment which superstition required him to wear in battle.

Onboard the German battlecruisers drums beat their crews to quarters as they followed Bödicker to the NW at 25 knots in the order *Lützow, Derfflinger, Seydlitz, Moltke* and *Von der Tann*, in the confident hope that they would soon cut off more British light cruisers than Sinclair's squadron. For Napier, whose Third Light Cruiser Squadron occupied stations next to the First Light Cruiser Squadron on Beatty's look-out screen, was not satisfied with the Commodore's concentration of four ships against Bödicker's four. Disregarding a pertinent warning in the *Grand Fleet Battle Orders*, he moved his squadron to Sinclair's support, thereby leaving a gap in the screen which was then unable to fulfil one of its *raisons d'être*: it gave Beatty no warning of Hipper's presence. At 1532 the *Lion* which had just altered course to E, and a little later the *Princess Royal*, 'sighted the enemy, five battlecruisers faintly distinguishable a very long distance away accompanied by some torpedo craft. First of all their smoke, and later the outline of their masts, funnels and the upper parts of the hulls became visible from the control position aloft, but from the turrets only smoke could be observed until some while later.' Fortunately the enemy ships were 14 miles away, still just outside gun range, for, although the German Admiral suffered the same disadvantage for the valid reason that he had fewer cruisers to form his screen, the lighter western horizon had enabled him to sight the British battlecruisers 12 minutes earlier.

Hipper reported the sighting to Scheer who immediately ordered his battleships to increase to their maximum station-keeping speed of 16 knots: Hipper also recalled Bödicker's squadron and, realizing his dangerous position, swung his five battlecruisers round to SSE. He aimed to lead his opponent, whose six battlecruisers were apparently being followed by five battleships, towards Scheer's Battle Fleet. (Hipper was under the false impression that all five 'Queen Elizabeths' were present; so, consequently, was Scheer.) Beatty likewise reported the enemy to his Commander-in-Chief as he closed the range at 25 knots with small regard for Evan-Thomas whose ships could only manage 24. At 1545, following detailed reports from the *Galatea* and *Falmouth*, whose squadrons were fulfilling their role of keeping in touch with the enemy, to the effect that Hipper had turned to SSE, Beatty altered to the converging course of ESE. Hipper deliberately withheld his fire since a close-range fight would reduce the odds against his fewer ships, of which three had only 11-inch guns. He could not, however, understand why the British ships withheld theirs for so long after the *Lion* was within the greater range of her 13·5-inch guns (23,000 yards). In fact, although Beatty's orders specified 16,000 yards as the best range 'to utilize the advantage of our heavier projectiles, to minimize the disadvantage of our lighter protection, [and because it] is inside the maximum range of our 12-inch guns', he waited for too long because conditions were so adverse that his ships over-estimated the range by more than 2,000 yards. When, at 1549, the range came down to 15,000 yards, it was Hipper's ships that first opened fire, though they nullified this advantage by also over-estimating the range. To quote von Hase, Gunnery Officer of the *Derfflinger*: 'The second salvo crashed out. Again it was over. "Down 400", I ordered. The third and fourth salvoes were also over although after the third I had given the order, "Down 800". "Good God, there's something wrong", I cursed; [and ordered] "Down 800" [again].' Hipper's decision obliged the British battlecruisers to open fire one minute after the German ships.

> Their salvoes gradually came closer [noted an officer in the *Princess Royal*] until, just as we saw the red-black burst of one of our shells hitting [the *Lützow*], we noticed the *Lion* ahead of us hit amidships [at 1551], and two minutes later we were hit by two 12-inch shells which temporarily knocked out our rangefinder tower. At 1556 the enemy were bearing about ten degrees abaft our beam, steering approximately south and both squadrons were firing on each other at a rate and with a determination that made one think that something big must happen in a few minutes.

A second hit on the *Lion* warned Beatty that 12,000 yards, at which the enemy ships could also use their secondary armaments, was too close, and he turned two points away just as Hipper altered to SE for the same reason.

An officer onboard the *New Zealand* near the rear of Beatty's line remembers that 'it was hard to believe that a battle was actually commencing: it was so like [an] exercise the way in which we and the Germans turned up on to more or less parallel courses and waited for the range to close before letting fly at each other. It all seemed very cold-blooded and mechanical, no chance here of seeing red, merely a case of cool scientific calculation and deliberate gunfire.' But the bloody realities of a naval battle and the importance of the human element were soon stressed in the British vessels. Once the range had been found, the gunnery of the German ships, which had the advantage of the light and the leeward position so that their targets were more clearly visible against the brighter western sky and less obscured by smoke blowing across the range, was distinctly better. The *Lion* and *Tiger* were both hit three minutes after the Germans opened fire, whereas none of their ships was struck for another five minutes when a shell from the *Queen Mary* put one of the *Seydlitz*'s turrets out of action, killing most of its crew. Moreover, notwithstanding the lesson of the Dogger Bank action, there was confusion among Beatty's six battle-cruisers in selecting their targets from among Hipper's five: the *Derfflinger* was left unfired at for nearly ten minutes before the *Queen Mary* shifted to her and scored a hit. Such blows did not, however, compare with those suffered by Beatty's force. Lieutenant W. S. Chalmers, who was on the *Lion*'s bridge, recalls:

By 1600 we were at close grips with the enemy. His fire was phenomenally accurate. All around us huge columns of water higher than the funnels were being thrown up as the enemy shells plunged into the sea. Some curled over and deluged us with water. Occasionally, above the noise of battle, we heard the ominous hum of a shell fragment and caught a glimpse of polished steel as it flashed past the bridge. I glanced aft and saw one of our boats go up in a cloud of splinters. We hoped the enemy was being similarly punished but the five shadowy forms, with sporadic tongues of fire leaping from their guns, were apparently none the worse and we could not tell what damage we were doing to them as it was difficult to see the splashes of our shells in the white mist. At about this time a blood-stained Sergeant of Marines appeared on the bridge. He was hatless, his clothes were burnt and he seemed to be somewhat dazed. I asked him what was the matter; in a tired voice he replied: '"Q" turret has gone, sir. All the crew are killed, and we have flooded the magazine.' I looked over the bridge. The armoured roof of 'Q' turret had been folded back like an open sardine tin, thick yellow smoke was rolling up in clouds from the gaping hole and the guns were cocked up awkwardly in the air.

A shell from the *Lützow* had pierced the roof of the flagship's midship 13·5-inch gun turret, detonating inside and killing or mortally wounding the whole gunhouse crew. As in the *Seydlitz* at the Dogger Bank action, the explosion ignited cordite charges in the working chamber immediately below, from which the flash passed down the turret trunk to the magazine handing room. But before this

> Major F. J. W. Harvey, R.M.L.I., the officer-in-charge of 'Q' turret, with his dying breath gave the order to close the magazine doors and flood the magazine. By the time flash reached the handing room, the crew of the magazine had closed the doors; some were found afterwards with their hands on the door clips [but] their work was done. The action taken by the turret crew in response to [Major Harvey's] order saved the ship.

All but two of 'Q' turret's crew of close on 100 officers and men died in this disaster which will always be remembered for Harvey's splendid presence of mind. 'In the long, rough, glorious history of the Royal Marines there is no name and no deed which in its character and consequences ranks above this' (*Churchill*). He was the first of those who earned the Victoria Cross before the day was over.

Four minutes later Beatty's force suffered a much more serious loss from the same defect in design. An officer onboard the *New Zealand* saw

> the *Indefatigable* hit by two shells [from the *Von der Tann*], one on the forecastle and one on the fore turret. Both appeared to explode on impact. Then there was an interval of about thirty seconds; at the end the ship blew up, commencing from forward. The explosion started with sheets of flame followed by a dense, dark smoke cloud which obscured the ship from view. All sorts of stuff was blown into the air, a 50-ft. steamboat being blown up about 200 ft., apparently intact though upside down.

Since no one in the *Indefatigable*'s 'A' turret had time to close the magazine doors and flood the magazine, Captain Sowerby and all but two of his company of more than 1,000 officers and men were lost with their ship, whose destruction was observed by a large barque which, with all sails set, was caught between the two fleets. The feelings of her crew may be imagined.

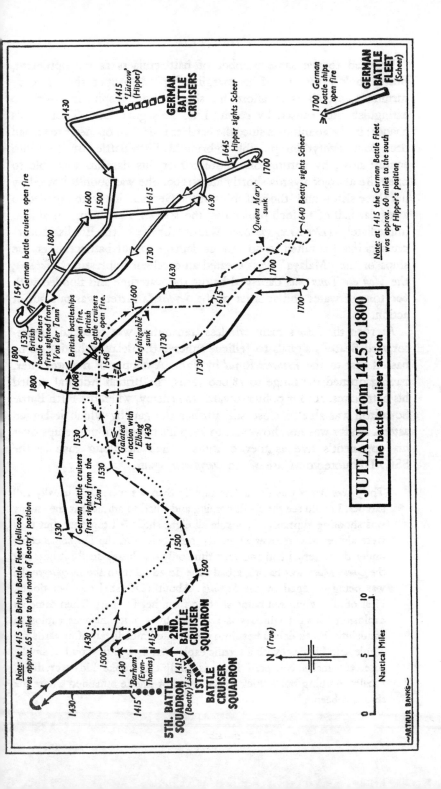

JUTLAND from 1415 to 1800
The battle cruiser action

Note: At 1415 the British Battle Fleet (Jellicoe) was approx. 65 miles to the north of Beatty's position.

Note: at 1415 the German Battle Fleet was approx. 60 miles to the south of Hipper's position.

GERMAN BATTLE CRUISERS

GERMAN BATTLE FLEET (Scheer)

1415 'Lützow' (Hipper)

1700 German battle ships open fire

German battle cruisers open fire

British battle cruisers first sighted from 'Von der Tann'

British battleships open fire. British battle cruisers open fire.

Hipper sights Scheer

1645 Hipper sights Scheer

'Queen Mary' sunk

1640 Beatty sights Scheer

'Indefatigable' sunk

'Galatea' in action with 'Elbing' at 1430

German battle cruisers first sighted from the 'Lion'

5TH. BATTLE SQUADRON

'Barham' (Evan-Thomas)

'Lion' (Beatty)

1ST. BATTLE CRUISER SQUADRON

2ND. BATTLE CRUISER SQUADRON

N (True)

Nautical Miles

0   5   10

ARTHUR BANKS

Reduced to the same number of battlecruisers as his opponent, Beatty took advantage of his margin of speed to open the range by turning away, so as to afford his ships a brief respite in which to extinguish fires caused by enemy hits. This gave Evan-Thomas his chance; in the 20 minutes since the battlecruisers had opened fire he had been doing everything possible to bring his Fifth Battle Squadron into action; now, by cutting one more corner, his flagship was able to open fire at 19,000 yards shortly after 1600. She was soon followed by her three sisters and 'the end ships of the German line were exposed to a regular hail of 15-inch projectiles, the *Von der Tann* being hit almost immediately' (*Der Krieg zur See*). Whilst 'the fire of the English battlecruisers [had] resulted in no serious damage to our battlecruisers, the ships of the "Malaya" class created an excellent impression' (*Scheer*); the *Von der Tann* was damaged below the waterline and flooded with 600 tons of water and another of the *Seydlitz*'s turrets was put out of action.

At 1610 the *Lion*'s main wireless transmitter was wrecked; henceforward Beatty's signals to Jellicoe suffered the delay of having to be passed first to the *Princess Royal* by light. A couple of minutes later, having opened the range to 18,000 yards, the British Admiral turned his battlecruisers four points towards the enemy, when the Fifth Battle Squadron was able to close still further the gap by which it lagged astern. Beatty was not, however, to keep his margin of nine ships over his opponent's five as they continued their headlong rush to the SSE. To quote von Hase of the *Derfflinger* again:

> The *Queen Mary* was firing less rapidly than we were, but usually full salvoes. I could see the shells coming and I had to admit that the enemy was shooting superbly. As a rule all eight shells fell together, but they were almost always over or short—only twice did the *Derfflinger* come under this infernal hail and each time only one heavy shell hit her. But the *Queen Mary* was having a bad time. In addition to the *Derfflinger* she was being engaged by the *Seydlitz*. About 1626 [she] met her doom. First of all a vivid red flame shot up from her forepart. Then came an explosion forward which was followed by a much heavier explosion amidships. Black debris flew into the air and immediately afterwards the whole ship blew up with a terrific explosion: a gigantic cloud of smoke rose, the masts collapsed inwards [and] the smoke hid everything. Finally, nothing but a thick, black cloud of smoke remained where the ship had been.

12 *The* Lion *is hit on* 'Q' *turret (amidships)*

13 *The British battlecruiser* Queen Mary *is destroyed by a salvo of heavy shell*

14   *Flagship of the Fifth Battle Squadron:* H.M.S. Barham *in Scapa Flow*

15   *Sunk at Jutland: the British armoured cruiser* Black Prince

An officer in the *New Zealand* noted:

> The *Tiger* was steaming at 24 knots only 500 yards astern of the *Queen Mary* and hauled sharply out of line to port and disappeared in this dense mass of smoke. We hauled out to starboard and passed the *Queen Mary* about 150 yards on our port beam, by which time the smoke had blown clear, revealing the stern from the funnel aft afloat and the propellers still revolving, but the forward part had already gone under. Men were crawling out of the top of the after turret, and up the after hatchway. When we were abreast, this after portion rolled over and blew up. Great masses of iron were thrown into the air and things were falling into the sea round us. Before we had quite passed, the *Queen Mary* completely disappeared.

Petty Officer E. Francis tells how he escaped from 'X' turret to be among the handful of survivors from Captain Prowse's crew of more than 1,000 officers and men:

> Then came the big explosion. Everything in the ship went as quiet as a church, the floor of the turret bulged up and the guns were useless. I put my head through the hole in the roof of the turret; the after 4-inch battery was smashed out of all recognition and the ship had an awful list to port. I told Lieutenant Ewart the state of affairs [and] he said, 'Clear the turret'. I went out through the top, followed by the Lieutenant. Suddenly he stopped and went back because he thought there was someone left inside. It makes one feel sore-hearted when I think of him and that fine crowd who were with me in the turret. I can only write about [their] splendid behaviour, but I am confident that the highest traditions of the Service were upheld by the remainder of the ship's company from the Captain down to the youngest boy. Everyone was so keen to be in a big fight. Two of my turret's crew, [with] no thought for their own safety, [helped me] gain the starboard side [where] there seemed to be quite a crowd [who] did not appear anxious to take the water, but something seemed to be urging me to get away. I must have covered nearly fifty yards when there was a big smash and the air seemed to be full of flying pieces. I heard a rush of water, which looked very much like surf breaking on a beach, and realized it was the suction or back-wash from the ship which had just gone. I hardly had time to fill my lungs when it was on me. [Though] I felt it was a losing game, I struck out and something bumped against me. I grasped it and found it was a large hammock [which] pulled me to the top more dead than alive. [Presently] I roused myself to look for something more substantial to support me, a piece of timber. My difficulty was to get on top and I was beginning to give up hope when the swell lifted me [there] and I must have become unconscious. When I came to my senses I was very sick and seemed to be full up with oil fuel. I managed to get [it] off my

face and eyes, which were aching awfully [and] looked around. Seeing no one else, I believed I was the only one left out of that fine ship's company. How long I was in the water before some destroyers came racing along I do not know [but] the *Petard* saw me [and] came up and a line was thrown to me which, needless to say, I grabbed hold of and was quickly hauled up on to her deck.

Beatty's courageous comment on seeing the second of his battle-cruisers so catastrophically destroyed has become a part of the Royal Navy's immortal tradition. To Chatfield he said without flinching, 'There seems to be something wrong with our bloody ships today'; as calmly he ordered a further alteration of course to enable his ships to 'engage the enemy more closely'. His officers and men were imbued with the same grim resolution: 'the spirits of our men were splendid', noted an officer in the *New Zealand*; 'in spite of the fact that they had plainly seen the *Queen Mary* blow up the idea of defeat did not seem to enter their heads.' At 1628 they had the satisfaction of seeing Hipper's line alter sharply away; the Germans were no longer able to stand up to the greater weight of British shellfire. 'It was nothing but the poor quality of the British bursting charges that saved us from disaster'* (*Hipper*). It is also arguable that it was Evan-Thomas's force that saved Beatty's battlecruisers. The latter had scored only ten hits on the enemy but had suffered 40 themselves, whereas they sustained no more during the remaining quarter of an hour of their run to the south while the guns of the Fifth Battle Squadron scored two hits on the *Moltke* and two on the *Von der Tann* in return for only one on the *Barham*.†

* This inexact criticism is explained on p. 160.

† As near as can be calculated the following is a summary of the hits suffered by both sides during the run south (approx. 55 minutes):

On British Ships	By German BCs	On German Ships	By British BCs	By British 5th B.S.
Lion	10	Lützow	4	
Princess Royal	2	Seydlitz	4	
Queen Mary	4 (sunk)	Von der Tann	1	2
Tiger	4	Moltke	1	2
Indefatigable	4 (sunk)			
Barham	2			
Warspite	3			
Malaya	3			
Total	32 (by 5 ships)	Total	10	4
			14 (by 10 ships)	

Hipper had another reason for altering course; if he was to lead the British force within range of Scheer's Battle Fleet he had to do more than survive the guns of the Fifth Battle Squadron. The way in which the two fleets had first made contact, coupled with Beatty's precipitate pursuit of his opponent, had made it difficult for the British destroyers to gain their proper position in the van; indeed, the smoke made by Commander Goldsmith's Ninth and Tenth Flotillas as they tried to achieve this by steaming at full speed between the lines contributed to the British battlecruisers' inaccurate gunfire. The Thirteenth Flotilla (less the *Onslow* and *Moresby* which were screening the *Engadine*) was, however, successful. At 1555 Beatty, with scant regard for the *Grand Fleet Battle Orders* to the effect that the chief duty of destroyers was to drive off enemy torpedoboats, had signalled, 'Opportunity appears favourable for attacking'; and by 1615 the *Champion* was sufficiently far ahead of the *Lion* for Captain Farie to release his eight destroyers, reinforced by four of Goldsmith's. These 12 boats carried out their attack in three divisions, led by the *Nestor*, Commander The Hon. E. B. S. Bingham, *Obdurate*, Lieutenant-Commander C. H. H. Sams, and *Narborough*, Lieutenant-Commander G. Corlett, 'in the most gallant manner and with great determination' (*Beatty*), for they did not have the sea to themselves. In response to an order received from Hipper at 1614, Heinrich in the *Regensburg* was leading Captain Goehle's Ninth Flotilla out to attack the British heavy ships; the result is described by an officer in H.M.S. *Nicator*, one of the *Nestor*'s division:

We led out from our battlecruiser line at 34 knots. Almost simultaneously we saw enemy torpedoboats coming out from the German line. When we had reached a position on the enemy's bow we turned and fired our first torpedo at 9,000 to 10,000 yards. By this time we were within gun range of the enemy torpedoboats approaching at about 30 knots, so we went into 'rapid independent' and scored a gratifying number of hits. We noticed that two of them stopped, one with a distinct list to starboard [the *V27* and *V29* subsequently sank] whilst the firing of the remainder was very wild and we were not hit at all. The *Nomad* astern of us was disabled by a hit in her engine-room and we had to leave her. All this time we were under an unpleasantly hot fire from the German battlecruisers' secondary armaments and it seemed nothing short of a miracle that we escaped being hit. I put it down to the way in which the Captain handled the ship: throughout the whole action [he] was leaning coolly against the front of the bridge smoking his pipe.

Both attacks were spoiled by this fierce clash in the 'no-man's-land' between the lines. Beatty and Evan-Thomas avoided all 18 torpedoes fired by Goehle's boats by temporarily turning their ships two points away. But although Hipper made a much larger turn to evade the 20 fired by Farie's destroyers, one from the *Petard*, Lieutenant-Commander E. C. O. Thomson, struck and flooded the *Seydlitz*, though not to such an extent as to reduce her speed and drive her out of the line.

The circumstances which prevented Captain Roper's First Flotilla and the bulk of Goldsmith's boats taking part in this attack had also resulted in Sinclair's and Napier's cruiser squadrons being left to the rear. But by 1620 Goodenough's Second Light Cruiser Squadron was able to reach a position from which to scout ahead of the British battlecruisers. Having by this time steamed some 50 miles towards the Horn Reefs since first sighting the enemy without contacting more than Hipper's ships, Beatty had every reason to believe the Admiralty's erroneous intelligence that this was the only enemy force at sea. If, on the other hand, Scheer had held his north-westerly course at 15 knots, giving a combined closing speed of 40, Beatty would have sighted him already. But the German Commander-in-Chief delayed the moment of meeting by steering W so that the British battlecruisers might be caught between his battleships and Hipper's force, until the *Frankfurt* reported the presence of the Fifth Battle Squadron. The German battle fleet, still in a long single line headed by Behncke's Battle Squadron, then turned back to NW in order to come to Hipper's support as quickly as possible. This enabled Hipper to achieve his purpose: 'We were about 1,500 yards ahead of our battlecruisers and 13,000 from the enemy', recalls Lieutenant Tennant* who was on the bridge of the *Nottingham*, 'when suddenly out of the mist on the port bow a line of big ships appeared. We stood on towards [them] with the rest of our squadron so as to be able to tell the Commander-in-Chief and the *Lion* exactly who was there.' At 1638 Jellicoe's and Beatty's illusion that Scheer's ships were at anchor in the Jade, was suddenly dispelled; from the *Southampton* came the electrifying news: 'Have sighted enemy battle fleet bearing SE, course N', followed a minute later by a similar report from the *Champion*. Beatty then knew that, all unwittingly, he had been led into a trap. He had been justly confident that, despite the loss of two battlecruisers, his remaining four, plus the Fifth Battle Squadron, would be able to cut off and destroy Hipper's five; now he had to

* Later Admiral Sir William Tennant (*vide* Acknowledgment).

escape from overwhelming force. He also had another duty, to lead the German Battle Fleet north until Scheer in his turn was trapped by Jellicoe's considerably superior Battle Fleet which was only 50 miles away.

So Beatty reacted to Goodenough's and Farie's reports by ordering his battlecruisers to reverse course, though he delayed the turn until 1640 when he could see for himself, 11 miles away to the SE, the masts and smoking funnels of Scheer's dreadnoughts showing above the horizon ahead of the *Lion*. As on previous occasions, notably when the *Galatea* first reported the enemy, Beatty turned his ships *in succession*: thereby he risked bringing the *Princess Royal*, *Tiger* and *New Zealand* as close to the enemy battle fleet as the *Lion* and, potentially more serious, of turning them round the same point on which the enemy might concentrate their fire. Fortunately Hipper was fully occupied with the Fifth Battle Squadron; moreover the *New Zealand*, at the tail of Beatty's line, finished turning before the head of the German battle fleet could come within range. It was a different story with the Fifth Battle Squadron. Beatty's signal, hoisted by flags at 1640, could not be read in the *Barham*, some seven miles away, and neither the *Tiger** nor the *Lion* passed it to her by light; so Evan-Thomas, again refusing to act without orders, continued to head for the enemy battle fleet. Six minutes after the *Lion* had turned Beatty repeated his signal, but again by flags which were not read by the *Barham* until the four battleships were abeam of the battlecruisers. Whilst the method by which the Fifth Battle Squadron altered course should have been left to Evan-Thomas to decide, Beatty courted disaster by specifying *in succession* instead of *together*. (This was one of the few criticisms which Jellicoe made of his conduct of the battle.) In view of the punishment his battlecruisers had suffered, Beatty intended that the Fifth Battle Squadron should become the main target for Hipper's gunfire; but by the time the *Barham* turned at 1657, a quarter of an hour after the *Lion*, she was within range of Scheer's battle fleet, and the fire of the German Third Battle Squadron was concentrated first on her, then on the *Valiant*, then on the *Warspite*, as each swung round the same pivotal point. Though Woolcombe's ship escaped damage, both Craig's and Phillpotts' received punishment. And 'when it was time for the

---

* It is not clear whether, after resuming a southerly course at 1430, Beatty expected her to re-assume duty as repeating ship (*vide* p. 72n).

Malaya to turn', wrote one of her officers, 'the turning point was a very hot corner. The shells were pouring in very fast and it is doubtful if we, the last ship of the line, could have got through without a severe hammering if the Captain [Boyle] had not used his initiative and turned the ship early.' Although the Fifth Battle Squadron thus drew the fire of the enemy battle fleet from Goodenough's light cruisers, their turn was a tactical error from which neither Beatty nor Evan-Thomas can be absolved.

The British battleships were saved from destruction by the stoutness of their armour and their skilful gunnery. After making his drastic turn away to avoid the Thirteenth Flotilla's torpedoes, Hipper had resumed his southerly course until 1645 when Scheer's Battle Fleet was sighted from the *Lützow*'s bridge. Twelve minutes later, and simultaneously with the Fifth Battle Squadron, Hipper made the same mistake as Beatty: he turned 16 points *in succession* to starboard so that his battlecruisers sustained further damage from the *Barham* and *Valiant*, and would have suffered more if the *Warspite* and *Malaya* had not had to turn their guns on to the head of Scheer's line.

> Very soon after the turn [noted the *Warspite*'s Executive Officer] I suddenly saw on the starboard quarter the whole of the High Seas Fleet; at least I saw masts, funnels and an endless ripple of orange flashes all down the line. The noise of their shells over and short was deafening, a frightful crack, crack, crack, going on all the time. I felt one or two heavy shakes but it never occurred to me that we were being hit. We were firing pretty fast on a bearing about Green 120 [thirty degrees abaft the starboard beam]. I distinctly saw two of our salvoes hit the leading German battleship. Sheets of yellow flame went right over her masthead, and she looked red fore and aft like a burning haystack.

The *König*, *Grosser Kurfürst* and *Markgraf* all received hits at about this time.

One minute after sighting the enemy battle fleet, Beatty had recalled Farie's destroyers. The *Obdurate*'s and *Narborough*'s divisions complied; so, initially did the *Nestor* and *Nicator*. According to the latter:

> On the way back we passed the *Nomad*, stopped and apparently helpless. We asked if we could offer any assistance but Lieutenant-Commander P. Whitfield told us to go on. Sighting a line of battleships on our port bow, I exclaimed: 'Now we're all right, here is the Fifth Battle Squadron.'

But that moment of elation did not last; a closer inspection showed they were Germans and *Nestor* was converging to attack them. Very soon we were again in the thick of a hair-raising bombardment. We were engaging a light cruiser at the head of the line with all our guns, the range on the sights being 3,000 yards: *Nestor* was apparently going to make certain of [this] attack. Just as our sights were coming on to an enemy battleship for our last torpedo, *Nestor* was hit and we had to put our helm hard-a-port to prevent ramming her. *Nestor*, realizing that he was out of action, ordered us to rejoin *Champion*, and accordingly we turned. The Captain [Lieutenant J. Mocatta] did not realize until afterwards that [our] torpedo had not been fired. In spite of the tornado of shells that were falling all around us, we were not hit once except by a few splinters.

But the damaged *Nestor* and *Nomad* could not escape:

A whole German battle squadron [wrote one of the latter's officers] was apparently using us as a target, [turning us] rapidly into something remarkably like Gruyère cheese. We were about 2,000 yards from the leading [one] when we fired our last torpedo, so were at practically point-blank range for their 11-inch and 12-inch guns. The ship started sinking by the stern and gradually disappeared, but all the men were got clear just before she sank and, after a short swim, a German torpedoboat picked us out of the water. We were taken back to Germany [to be] the Kaiser's 'guests' for the next two-and-a-half years.

Commander Bingham, who gained the V.C. for leading his division with such spirit, described the *Nestor*'s end in a letter to his wife written from Germany four days later:

Whitfield and I were left like little lambs directly in the path of the oncoming High Seas Fleet. There we lay for a few awful moments, the enemy masses looming up nearer and nearer [and] not a friend in sight. It was a relief when the shells arrived. I cleared away the boats. I could not retaliate, my guns were too small. Then the shells came, salvoes of enemy projectiles. I knew it was only a matter of a few minutes so I gave the order, 'Every man for himself'.

The First Lieutenant, M. J. Bethell, was standing beside his Captain. 'Now where shall *we* go?' Bingham asked him. 'To heaven, I trust, sir,' Bethell answered as, without thought for himself, he turned to tend a wounded man.

We took to the boats [Bingham's letter continues] and shoved off clear. [The *Nestor*] sank a few seconds after, stood up bows in the air, then dived stern first. We gave three cheers as she went down and then sang 'Tipperary' and 'The King'. [Later] a division of German destroyers came along and picked us up, 75 out of 83, who spent the rest of the battle like rats in a hole [below decks under guard] quite sure that British destroyers would come up and sink us. It tested our loyalty to the utmost to wish it so at the expense of our own lives. Can you picture our feelings every time the alarm gong rang and their guns barked? [However] the room was nice and warm, we were given food and wine, the [German] officers were very kind to us and nature came to my rescue and I slept!

The few who did not thus reach the safety of a prisoner-of-war camp included, alas, the gallant Bethell.

Goodenough turned a blind eye to Beatty's signal to reverse course. Not content with sighting the enemy, the Second Light Cruiser Squadron stood on to the SE until, from a range of 13,000 yards, the *Southampton* could report the formation and composition of Scheer's Battle Fleet and confirm its northerly course at 1700.

It was no good us engaging battleships with our 6-inch guns and so, having reported the enemy, the only thing we could do was to get away as quickly as possible. Shells burst close to the [*Nottingham*] and sent great fountains of water up the height of the mast. Others would burst 100 yards short and all the pieces came hurtling over our heads, some hitting the ship, but we had no casualties. All this time we were, needless to say, going full speed, and with the whole German Fleet following it is fortunate that nothing went wrong down in the engine-room. (*Lieutenant Tennant*)

Before the day was done Goodenough, now following the Fifth Battle Squadron to the north, was to do more than this classic piece of cruiser work to wipe from the slate the mistake he had made on 16th December 1914. Some 300 miles away to the SW Tyrwhitt, lying in Harwich Harbour, reacted to Goodenough's report with a pointed request for 'instructions' from the Admiralty. The response was an order to complete with fuel: 'you may have to relieve light cruisers and destroyers in Battlecruiser Fleet later'. This, however, crossed further word from Tyrwhitt; unable to restrain his desire to help Beatty, he signalled at 1715: 'I am proceeding to sea'. His chagrin 20 minutes later when the Admiralty retorted, 'Return at once and await orders', was only exceeded by his later realization, when he was eventually allowed to sail after dawn on 1st June, that his five light cruisers and 19 destroyers could play no part. The First Sea Lord thought that Tyrwhitt's ships should be held back in case Scheer detached a part of his fleet to make a raid on shipping in the Downs. On the other hand, although the Harwich Force could have joined up with Jellicoe before the night, it is doubtful whether it would have made any significant difference to the outcome of the battle.

The British Commander-in-Chief's immediate reaction to the *Galatea*'s first enemy report had been to order steam for full speed. This had enabled him to increase to 18 knots at 1455, and to 20 by 1600. Steering S50E, his battleships could do no more than this, their maximum station-keeping speed, to close the distance which separated them from Beatty—which was some 12 miles more than planned because Jellicoe had likewise been delayed for the best part of an hour by the need to search trawlers suspected of using their wireless to report British warships to Germany. At 1510, however, Jellicoe had ordered Arbuthnot's and Heath's cruiser squadrons, which were spread as a look-out line ahead of the *Iron Duke*, to increase their distance to 16 miles (though they had little margin of speed to achieve this in the time available). More important, the Third Battlecruiser Squadron, with its accompanying light cruisers *Chester* and *Canterbury* and four destroyers, had increased to 22 knots, bent on rejoining the Battlecruiser Fleet to which Hood's ships properly belonged. This initiative was confirmed by Jellicoe at 1605. Twenty-five minutes later the bugles of the British battleships summoned officers and men to their action stations. They were there when Jellicoe received Good-enough's report giving the unexpected but very welcome news that Scheer's Battle Fleet was only 50 miles way. By 1700 the Admiralty received the signal for which they had been waiting for nearly two years: 'Fleet action is imminent'.

To allow Jellicoe to make contact with Scheer and to ensure that the High Seas Fleet was unable to escape by precipitate flight as it had so often done before, Beatty had to get far enough ahead of Hipper to force the German battlecruisers round to the east, thereby preventing them from giving Scheer warning of the British Battle Fleet's approach. For this reason the British battlecruisers, after turning to NNW, maintained their speed of 25 knots so that by 1710 they had drawn out of range of Hipper's force. The slightly slower Fifth Battle Squadron continued in action for some 20 minutes longer, both with Hipper's battlecruisers and with the German First and Third Battle Squadrons which had increased to 20 knots, leaving Mauve's pre-dreadnoughts behind. But, though these four British battleships were targets for German dreadnoughts for nearly half an hour, Scheer's 'hope that one would be so damaged as to fall a prey to our main fleet was not fulfilled'; none fared worse than the *Malaya* which had two holes below the waterline and her starboard 6-inch battery wrecked with heavy casualties. Their 15-inch guns, on the other hand, scored effective hits on the *Grosser Kurfürst*, *Markgraf*, *Seydlitz* and the already crippled *Lützow*, whilst the *Derfflinger* suffered damage below the waterline. Assuredly Evan-Thomas's ships were stoutly built and stoutly manned, but Scheer's failure to do them more damage is a reflection on his battle fleet's gunnery; Behncke's and Schmidt's squadrons did not show the same skill as Hipper's in the first half-hour of their action with Beatty.

> The Fifth B.S. were a brave sight [wrote Lieutenant Stephen King-Hall,* who was in the *Southampton*]. They were receiving the concentrated fire of some twelve German heavy ships but it did not seem to be worrying them and the German shooting did not impress me very favourably. But our own position was not pleasant. The half-dozen older battleships at the tail of the German line were too far away to fire at the Fifth B.S. and, though we had gradually drawn out to 15,000 or 16,000 yards, we were inside their range and they began to do target practice on our squadron. I was in the after control with half a dozen men. We crouched down behind the tenth-of-an-inch plating and ate bully beef; but it seemed rather a waste of time, for surely in the next ten minutes one of those 11-inch shells would get us; they couldn't go on falling just short and just over indefinitely.

But they did; the captains of Goodenough's highly manœuvrable squadron avoided being hit by constantly altering course towards each enemy salvo as it fell short or over on the sound principle that it was unlikely that two successive ones would fall in the same place. The success of this may be judged from Scheer's irritable comment: 'Their vague and purposeless hurrying to and fro led one to think that our fire had so surprised them that they did not know which way to turn next.'

Two much smaller ships harried the German Battle Fleet. Having missed their flotilla's attack, the destroyers *Onslow*, Lieutenant-Commander J. C. Tovey,† and *Moresby*, Lieutenant-Commander R. V.

---

* Later Sir Stephen King-Hall, founder of the Hansard Society.

† Later Admiral of the Fleet Lord Tovey, Commander-in-Chief Home Fleet during part of the Second World War.

Alison, were released from screening the *Engadine*. At 1700 Tovey found himself closing an enemy who appeared to have no torpedoboat screen. The opportunity was too good to miss: he led the *Moresby* in. Before the two boats could get within torpedo range they ran into Reuter's Fourth Scouting Group whose heavy fire compelled them to turn away. Tovey swung the *Onslow* to port and abandoned his attack, but Alison, swinging the *Moresby* to starboard, found another opening and was able to fire a torpedo at the *Kronprinz Wilhelm*, third ship in Scheer's line, at a range inside 8,000 yards. Though this gallant effort failed, Alison handled his ship so well that she emerged unscathed from the hail of enemy shell which pursued her.

At 1730 Beatty, who no longer had Hipper in sight, judged the time opportune for his purpose and swung his battlecruisers round to NNE. Almost at the same time Scheer, believing that his opponent was escaping him, ordered his battlecruisers 'to give chase'; Hipper therefore altered to NW with the intention of renewing the action. As a result, some ten minutes later, the German battlecruisers were engaged both by Beatty's from right ahead and by the Fifth Battle Squadron on their starboard bow. This left Hipper no alternative but to turn away; he tried to limit this to 45 degrees but by 1755 the fire from eight British heavy ships, which had the advantage of the better light previously held by their opponents whose gunlayers were now dazzled by the setting sun, had inflicted fresh damage on the German battlecruisers. The *Lützow* was heavily hit, the *Derfflinger* was holed and flooded forward and the *Seydlitz* set on fire.* This compelled Hipper to turn right away.

* For comparison with the footnote to p. 84, the following is a summary of hits scored after the British ships began their turn to the north (approx. 75 minutes):

	ON BRITISH SHIPS			ON GERMAN SHIPS	
	By German BCs	By German 3rd BS		By British BCs	By British 5th BS
Lion	2		Lützow	2	4
Barham		4	Derfflinger	1	3
Malaya		4	Seydlitz	2	4
Warspite		5	Grosser Kurfürst ⎱		1
			Markgraf ⎰		2
			König		1
Total	2	13	Total	5	15

15 (by about 10 ships)   20 (by 8 ships)

The superiority of the Fifth Battle Squadron's gunnery over that of the British battlecruisers reflects, among other factors, the lack of adequate practice facilities in the Firth of Forth compared with Scapa Flow.

By 1800, when he was as much as six miles on Scheer's starboard bow because his Commander-in-Chief had given up his chase after Evan-Thomas and reduced speed to 15 knots to allow Mauve's squadron to catch up, the German battlecruisers were in full flight to the east.

Beatty thus prevented Hipper from sighting and giving Scheer warning of the presence of Jellicoe's force and ensured that the two Battle Fleets, which were now only just over the horizon from each other, would make contact. How this came about is best left to a fresh chapter; this may fittingly conclude with an assessment of how much both battle-cruiser Admirals had achieved.

The initial advantage had gone to Hipper: he had lured a much superior British force within range of Scheer's Battle Fleet and, in the process, sunk a third of his opponents' battlecruisers. His success is not diminished by Beatty's tactical mistake, made the worse by a signal error, which for a time denied him the support of the powerful Fifth Battle Squadron, nor by the British battlecruisers' poor shooting. But he who gains first points is not necessarily the victor. Since the British had had as many as nine battlecruisers (plus two in dockyard hands) against the High Seas Fleet's five (plus one nearing completion), the loss of two was not of great consequence. Nor had these disasters deterred Beatty from pursuing his opponent until he could report the presence of Scheer's Battle Fleet to Jellicoe. If by a second tactical mistake, again aggravated by a signal error, he had needlessly en-dangered the Fifth Battle Squadron, these vessels had used their 15-inch guns to such effect that Hipper's ships had suffered much heavier damage than any of the surviving British ones. Two had been seriously holed below the waterline and flooded, whilst the *Von der Tann* had all her main armament out of action, though Captain Zenker, to his credit, had kept his place in the line 'so that the enemy, having to take his ship into account, would not be able to strengthen his fire against the other battlecruisers' (*Der Krieg zur See*). Finally Beatty had done more than elude the whole strength of the High Seas Fleet; he had out-manœuvred Hipper so that Scheer was, without premonition of his fate, about to meet the superior force which it was his aim to avoid.

There is, therefore, no question about Beatty's success in outwitting his opponents and achieving the purpose expected of his Battlecruiser Fleet. By 1800 the advantage was with the British. Whether this would result in victory remained to be decided by Jellicoe and Scheer. The former had the more powerful fleet, but over its prospects hung a cloud more menacing than the mist and smoke of battle which now restricted the visibility to less than six miles. Initial contact between the two fleets had not been made until half-way through the afternoon so that less than three hours remained before a summer night would cast its cloak of darkness across the North Sea.*

* Sunset was shortly after 2000.

4

'Equal Speed Charlie London'

'Suddenly the German van was faced by the belching guns
of an interminable line of heavy ships.'

Der Kreig zur See

'That terrible day when we might have accomplished so
much.'

Admiral Beatty to his wife

IT IS NOT easy to present a coherent account of the next phase of the
action since so much of consequence occurred more or less simultaneously around 1800. But there is no doubt as to which incident was
most important; before Jellicoe could engage Scheer he had to deploy
his ships into line of battle. Britain's admirals had learned that Nelson's
dictum, 'the order of sailing is to be the order of battle', though
proper for ships-of-the-line which were subject to the vagaries of the
wind, did not apply to steam-driven ironclads. The need for a ship's
length to be greater than its beam dictated the broadside mounting of
multi-gunned armaments in the days of sail. A similar rule applied
with the advent of turrets; dreadnoughts could only bring the maximum
number of heavy guns to bear if their 'A arcs' were open (*i.e.* if the
enemy was between about 50 degrees before and 50 degrees abaft the
beam). A fleet could likewise only develop its maximum weight of fire
if individual ships avoided masking each others' 'A arcs', so that its
'order of battle' had to approximate to line ahead. But since an enemy
would normally be sighted well before the beam, this formation was
not suitable for the approach; the necessary alteration of course in
succession, to port or starboard, to open 'A arcs' would take about
20 minutes during which the enemy could concentrate a dangerous
weight of fire on the turning point. The theoretically ideal 'order of

sailing' was line abreast because all ships could be quickly deployed into line by altering course together; but in other respects this was a too clumsy formation. The adopted solution was a compromise: the battle fleet which Jellicoe led south to Beatty's support was in six columns, each of four ships in line ahead, whose leaders were disposed abeam. Jerram in the *King George V* led the port wing column; the other half of the Second Battle Squadron formed the next, led by Rear-Admiral Leveson in the *Orion*. Jellicoe himself headed the third column in the *Iron Duke*; four more ships of the Fourth Battle Squadron headed by Sturdee in the *Benbow*, comprised the fourth. The fifth column was led by Rear-Admiral Gaunt in the *Colossus*; Jellicoe's second-in-command, Burney, in the *Marlborough*, led the other half of the First Battle Squadron on the starboard wing.

Much thought and many exercises had been devoted to the problem of how to deploy a fleet thus formed (*i.e.* to bring it into line ahead with all ships' 'A arcs' open), so as to complete the manœuvre to best tactical advantage before the enemy could open fire. Both the method and direction of the deployment depended upon the bearing of the centre of the enemy fleet. So long as gun ranges were of the order of 4,000–6,000 yards, there was ample time for an admiral to make this decision after he had sighted the enemy for himself; but when Jellicoe assumed command ships might open fire at near-horizon range, so that his fleet had to be deployed whilst the enemy was well beyond this. He depended upon his advanced forces supplying him with the enemy's bearing and distance, formation, course and speed.

Unfortunately, although the *Grand Fleet Battle Orders* emphasized the need for adequate enemy reports, the majority of Jellicoe's admirals and captains failed to signal them at Jutland. After Sinclair's initial ones around 1430, the British Commander-in-Chief heard nothing until Napier's just after 1500. No further reports of Hipper's ships were made until Beatty, Goodenough and Napier signalled them around 1540. Fifteen minutes later Beatty added that he was in action, but Evan-Thomas remained silent so that Jellicoe had to wireless him at 1617: 'Are you in company with Senior Officer Battlecruiser Fleet?', to which he received the somewhat ambiguous reply: 'I am engaging the enemy'. None of this, for which both Beatty and Evan-Thomas had the excuse that his flagship's wireless was out of action, might be of great importance since Scheer's Battle Fleet had not been sighted. It was a different matter when Goodenough made his report at 1638, closely followed by Farie, and at 1645 by Beatty (though this was mangled and delayed in transmission through the *Princess Royal*), whereby Jellicoe learned that, contrary to the Admiralty's intelligence, the German Battle Fleet was no more than 50 miles away. He was now vitally concerned with the problem of on which column and on what course he should deploy. But, after the admirable reports made by Goodenough at 1648 and 1700, he heard nothing until the Commodore reported again 40 minutes later, except for wireless bearings of the enemy at 1609 (signalled by the Admiralty at 1700) and at 1630 (likewise signalled at 1745) which suggested that he would sight the enemy approximately ahead. Thus Scheer's bearing and distance from the *Iron Duke* remained far from clear when Jellicoe was closing his opponent at a combined speed of 40 knots.

At 1730, when Beatty swung his battlecruisers followed by the Fifth Battle Squadron round to NNE to lead Hipper away from the British Battle Fleet, the *Falmouth*, stationed four miles to the north of the *Lion*, sighted the *Black Prince* on the starboard wing of Jellicoe's cruiser screen, which had managed to get about eight miles ahead since 1510. This first visual link between the two British forces should have given Jellicoe much of the information he needed, but Napier only signalled, 'Battlecruisers engaged to SSW', which Bonham passed to the *Iron Duke* in the inaccurate form, 'Enemy battlecruisers bearing S five miles', information so unlikely that it was rejected in the fleet flagship. Subsequent reports from the *Southampton*, *Black Prince* and *Defence* were no more helpful so that Jellicoe was left in suspense until 1750 when both the *Lion* and *Barham* were sighted by Burney, who reported their bearings from the *Marlborough*. This disclosed the disturbing fact that there were differences in the navigational reckonings of Jellicoe's and Beatty's flagships; the *Lion* was 11 miles nearer the *Iron Duke* and on a more westerly bearing than where the Commander-in-Chief had supposed her to be. Consequently Jellicoe would sight Scheer's battle fleet 20 minutes earlier than he had expected, so that he had that much less time in which to deploy and to order his destroyers to proceed ahead ready to counter an enemy torpedoboat attack—all too little time when he still lacked the most vital piece of information, the bearing of his opponent's flagship.

'Large masses of smoke from the hundreds of ships making at full speed for the scene of the battle lay between the lines [drifting] to the NE, where they combined to form an impenetrable pall, pierced here and there by the flash of salvoes, the detonation of hitting shells and flames from fires and explosions' (*Der Krieg zur See*). Jellicoe's spearhead, the Third Battlecruiser Squadron, which had been pressing ahead since 1510, had done nothing to pierce this fog because Hood had chosen a south-south-easterly course so that he might cut off any enemy force which tried to escape into the Skagerrak. This took him to the eastward of Hipper's ships until 1730 when Captain Lawson of the light cruiser *Chester*, stationed six miles to starboard of the *Invincible*, sighted gun flashes to the SW and turned to investigate.

> In a very short time [one of her officers] sighted light cruisers on the port bow steering approximately NNW. Seen dimly through the mist they appeared not unlike our own First Light Cruiser Squadron. We altered parallel to them [and] almost immediately saw the flash of gunfire ripple along the side of the [*Frankfurt*, in which Bödicker was leading the Second Scouting Group ahead of Hipper's battlecruisers]. The enemy's first salvo fell a good 2,000 yards beyond us, the second 500 to 700 yards short, and most of the third came onboard, a very good bit of target finding. A few seconds before this we had [fired] our first salvo, and it was our last, for the majority of the guns' crews and all the voice-pipes and electrical communications were smashed up by the [enemy] salvo. [With] the whole of the enemy squadron concentrating on us the odds were more than we could stand and the Captain decided to fall back on the Third Battlecruiser Squadron. We altered to NE which brought our opponents astern and zigzagged to dodge [their] salvoes. Fortunately no part of the engine-room or boilers was damaged and when we rang down for emergency full speed, the engineers worked up to 28 knots. By this good work we gradually increased our range from the enemy [until] we passed ahead of the *Invincible*. The number of direct hits received was 18, but we were also hit by a large amount of splinters from shells bursting in the water. The engine-room mascot, a black kitten, was taken below when action was sounded and apparently did its duty nobly!

The *Chester*'s casualties during this brief engagement against fourfold odds, from which Lawson so skilfully extricated his ship, included the sight-setter of the forecastle gun, Boy First Class John Travers Cornwell.

> Mortally wounded early in the action, he nevertheless remained standing alone at a most exposed post quietly awaiting orders with the gun's crew dead and wounded all round him. His age was under 16½ years. I [Beatty] regret that he has since died, but I recommend his case for

16 *The deed for which Boy John Cornwell (aged 16), of* H.M.S. Chester, *was awarded the Victoria Cross*
(From the painting by Sir Frank Salisbury)

17 *The midship magazines of the British battlecruiser* Invincible *explode*

18 *The wreck of the* Invincible, *with the destroyer* Badger *picking up the few survivors*

special recognition in justice to his memory and as an acknowledgment of the high example set by him.

Cornwell was awarded a posthumous V.C.

For Bödicker Nemesis was near; as soon as he heard the *Chester*'s gunfire, Hood turned his three battlecruisers towards her.

> At 1755 *Invincible* opened fire and was followed five minutes later by *Inflexible* and *Indomitable* [recalls one of the latter's officers]. We could see [the *Chester*] off the port bow heavily engaged with a squadron of enemy light cruisers. Our opening range was 11,200 yards, closing to 8,000. We steamed between our own light cruisers and the enemy [ships] and severely handled them, one disappearing in a great cloud of steam and smoke, whilst another was badly on fire amidships and apparently stopped.

British guns reduced the *Wiesbaden* to a smoking wreck, cut the *Pillau*'s speed to 24 knots and severely damaged the *Frankfurt*. Bödicker's squadron was only saved from annihilation by the appearance of a more powerful German force, Hipper's battlecruisers being headed clear of Jellicoe's Battle Fleet by Beatty's ships. Believing the *Invincible* and her sisters to be battleships—a mistake also made by Bödicker whose reports encouraged Scheer to believe that he was about to cut off a division of British battleships in addition to Beatty's and Evan-Thomas's squadrons—Hipper ordered his torpedoboats to attack, and swung his main force away to the SW, whereby he soon came in sight of Behncke's Third Battle Squadron coming NNE, and was able to turn into his station ahead of Scheer's Battle Fleet.

The torpedo attack on the Third Battlecruiser Squadron was attempted by the *Regensburg* and 31 torpedoboats from the Second, Sixth and Ninth Flotillas. But Heinrich's boats only managed to fire 12 torpedoes which the British ships avoided by turning away—'one passed under the [*Indomitable*], one passed ahead, one a few yards astern, and one was observed running slowly down the starboard side a few yards off'—because Hood ordered his four destroyers to counter-attack.

> Led by Commander Loftus Jones in the *Shark*, the division hurled itself at the German force, opening fire with every gun that would bear. In spite of their numerical superiority the German destroyers turned away in the face of this determined onslaught. [But] three [enemy] battle-cruisers appeared out of the mist, and the gallant division [came] under a deluge of shells. A projectile struck the *Shark*'s wheel, shattering it and wounding the Coxswain, Petty Officer Griffin. The Captain ordered the

after wheel to be manned and followed the Coxswain down the ladder to the shell-torn upper deck. Wounded in the thigh and face, endeavouring to stanch the flow of blood with his hands, [Loftus Jones found] that a shell had burst inside the engineroom, the main engines and steering gear [being] disabled. Lieutenant-Commander J. O. Barron gallantly brought *Acasta* between her and the enemy's fire, and signalled to ask if he could be of assistance. The Captain of the *Shark* replied: 'No. Tell him to look after himself and not get sunk over us', [so] the *Acasta* followed in the wake of the other two boats [as they] rejoined the battlecruisers [which] vanished into the mist.

The enemy [then] closed in upon the *Shark* [which] was settling by the bows and every minute shuddered with the impact of a fresh hit. One by one the wounded crawled into the lee of the casings and funnels in a pitiful attempt to find shelter. The Captain ordered the collision-mats to be placed over the shot-holes and every attempt made to keep the ship afloat. The Coxswain, though half-blinded by blood, superintended a party turning out boats and rafts. The midship gun under Midshipman T. Smith, R.N.R., maintained a steady fire [with] the crew reduced to two men. [When] Able Seaman Howell, who had been severely wounded, dropped from loss of blood, the Captain took his place. A moment later a shell took off his right leg above the knee.

As his strength ebbed Commander Loftus Jones seems to have been overtaken by fear lest the ship should fall into the hands of the enemy. He asked faintly what had happened to the flag. One of the men tending him replied that it had been shot away, and in great distress he ordered another to be hoisted. Seeing it once more flying clear, [he] said: 'That's good'. [But] the end was drawing near. The bows of the *Shark* had sunk until the waves were lapping over the waterlogged hull, [and since] two German destroyers had approached with the intention of administering the *coup de grâce,* Commander Loftus Jones gave his last order: 'Save yourselves!'. He was helped into the water and floated clear with the support of a lifebelt [whilst] the remainder of the crew, about a score, swam towards the rafts and pieces of floating wreckage. Two torpedoes struck the *Shark* amidships and she sank with colours flying about an hour and a half after firing her first shot. [When] the battlecruisers swept past in pursuit of the enemy, the Captain asked if they were British. Stoker Petty Officer Filleul replied that they were and the Captain said, 'That's good!' [Then] his head fell forward and his gallant spirit fled. ('*Bartimeus*')

Shortly after midnight, several of the *Shark*'s magnificent company were picked up by a Danish steamer. One died of exhaustion before she reached port; the courage of the others was acknowledged by the award of Distinguished Service Medals. A few weeks later the body of Commander Loftus Jones, whose heroism was soon recognized by the Victoria Cross, was washed ashore on the coast of Sweden, to be buried with a stone at his head and his feet, Viking fashion, in the village churchyard of Fiskebackskil.

In contrast to the reports made to Scheer by Bödicker and Hipper, none of this activity was signalled to Jellicoe. He was left to wonder whether the sound of the Third Battlecruiser Squadron's gunfire, heard on the *Iron Duke*'s port bow, could be the bearing of Scheer's battle fleet which he so badly needed. Fortunately this did not fit with his other information, so that he rejected it, because at 1801 (as Jellicoe's Flag Captain, Dreyer, recalls) 'Beatty appeared out of the mist on [the *Iron Duke*'s] starboard bow, leading his splendid battle-cruisers which were engaged to starboard with an enemy invisible to us. I noted smoke pouring from a shell-hole on the port side of the *Lion*'s forecastle and grey, ghost-like columns of water thrown up by heavy enemy shells pitching among these great ships'. Immediately Jellicoe flashed: 'Where is the enemy battle fleet?' At 1803 Good-enough wirelessed that he had lost touch with Scheer; so had Beatty, who therefore answered, at 1806, 'Enemy *battlecruisers* bearing SE'. Desperately Jellicoe repeated his question. Fortunately the mist to the south of the *Lion* lifted at 1810:

> I [Dreyer] was watching the steering of the ship when I heard the signalman calling Beatty's reply: 'Have sighted enemy battle fleet bearing SSW' [*i.e.* on the *Iron Duke*'s starboard bow]. I then heard the sharp, distinctive step of the Commander-in-Chief. He looked in silence at the magnetic compass for about 20 seconds. I watched his keen, brown, weatherbeaten face, wondering what he would do. He was as cool and unmoved as ever. Then he looked up and broke the silence with the order to Commander A. R. W. Woods, the Fleet Signal Officer: 'Hoist equal speed pendant south-east'. Woods said: 'Would you make it a point to port, sir, so that they will know it is on the port wing column?' Jellicoe replied: 'Very well. Hoist equal speed pendant south-east-by-east'. Woods then called over the bridge rail to the Signal Boatswain: 'Hoist Equal Speed Charlie London'.* The signal was made by wireless at the same time [1815].

This required Jerram's column, led by the *King George V*, to alter course no more than a few degrees to port in succession. By swinging some 70 degrees to port together the other column leaders, as soon as

---

* The flags 'CL' were the code group for SEbyE.

their divisions had followed them round, brought the fleet into line ahead; a further turn in succession to starboard in Jerram's wake formed the fleet into its 'order of battle'—single line ahead, course SEbyE. 'I was guided in my deployment by two factors: one was to "cross the T"; two, to get the best light for gunnery'. But Jellicoe had achieved more than this: he had put the British Battle Fleet on to a course which led between the High Seas Fleet and its base.

A very great sailor, Admiral of the Fleet Lord Cunningham, who was not at Jutland, wrote that, if he had been in command of the Grand Fleet, 'I hope I would have been given the good sense to make the same deployment'. Despite the difficult circumstances, Jellicoe's clear brain had made a decision which brought his fleet into line ahead by 1820, albeit with a bend of some 110 degrees in it, but *concave* to the enemy so that all ships could bring their guns to bear over a wide arc. He has, however, been criticized on the score that it led to an artillery duel at too great a range. In fact it was soon inside 10,000 yards; moreover, the alternative of deployment on the starboard wing would have produced a bend *convex* to the enemy (unless Jellicoe had sacrificed the advantage of the easterly position), masking the fire of many British ships for some 20 vital minutes. More reasonably, it has been suggested that Jellicoe should have deployed on a centre column because, if the *Iron Duke* had continued to steer SE, with the other battleships forming astern of her division, Jellicoe would have achieved his aims *and* engaged Scheer at a more effective range. But although the possible need for this, especially when an enemy was sighted with little warning, had been considered before the war, it had been rejected, chiefly because experience showed that an admiral could better control his fleet from the centre than the van. Churchill's statement in *The World Crisis*, that an ordinary 'forming and disposing signal' could have been used is a half-truth: it would have thrown the British battle fleet into disorder, with half the ships masking the guns of the others when they were within range of Scheer's line. But, 'the battle did not hinge upon whether Jellicoe deployed on the starboard or port wing column, but upon how firmly his determination was set upon destroying the enemy and obtaining a decisive victory' (*Richmond*).

Because Jellicoe's deployment was delayed, much happened in the rapidly narrowing area between the two fleets across which Jellicoe's

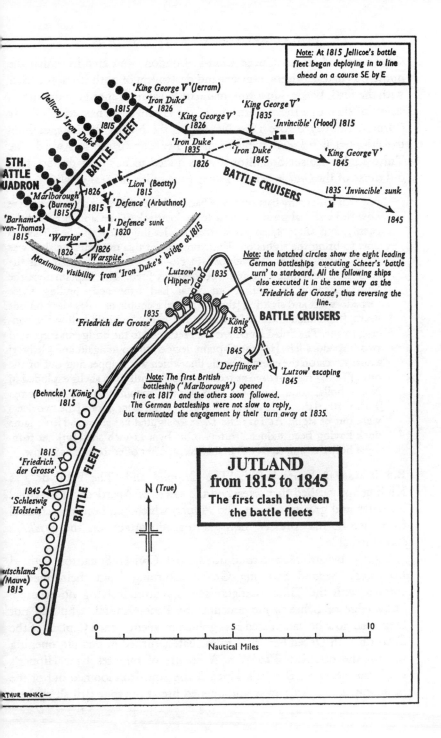

Note: At 1815 Jellicoe's battle fleet began deploying in to line ahead on a course SE by E

'King George V' (Jerram)
'Iron Duke' 1826
'King George V' 1826
'King George V' 1835
'Invincible' (Hood) 1815
'Iron Duke' 1835
'Iron Duke' 1845
'King George V' 1845

(Jellicoe) 'Iron Duke'

BATTLE FLEET

1815
1815
1815

5TH. BATTLE SQUADRON

1835 'Invincible' sunk
1845

BATTLE CRUISERS

1826
'Lion' (Beatty) 1815
'Defence' (Arbuthnot)
1826
1815
'Defence' sunk 1820

'Marlborough' (Burney) 1815

'Barham' (Evan-Thomas) 1815

'Warrior'
1826
'Warspite'

Maximum visibility from 'Iron Duke's' bridge at 1815

Note: the hatched circles show the eight leading German battleships executing Scheer's 'battle turn' to starboard. All the following ships also executed it in the same way as the 'Friedrich der Grosse', thus reversing the line.

'Lutzow' (Hipper)
1835

1835
'Friedrich der Grosse'

'König 1835'

BATTLE CRUISERS

1845
'Derfflinger'
'Lutzow' escaping 1845

Note: The first British battleship ('Marlborough') opened fire at 1817 and the others soon followed. The German battleships were not slow to reply, but terminated the engagement by their turn away at 1835.

(Behncke) 'König' 1815

BATTLE FLEET

1815
'Friedrich der Grosse'

1845
'Schleswig Holstein'

N (True)

'Deutschland' (Mauve) 1815

| JUTLAND |
| from 1815 to 1845 |
| The first clash between |
| the battle fleets |

0   5   10
Nautical Miles

ARTHUR BANKS—

ships executed 'Equal Speed Charlie London'—an area in which the numerous battlecruisers, cruisers and destroyers of both sides, together with the Fifth Battle Squadron, manœuvred at high speed amidst such a storm of shell that the wardrooms of the Grand Fleet named it 'Windy Corner'. Shortly before 1800 Napier, to the NE of the *Lion*, sighted the crippled *Wiesbaden* trying to make her way to the westward; the Third Light Cruiser Squadron's guns added to her damage. So, too, did those of the *Onslow* before Tovey (one of his officers recalls)

> saw that the enemy battlecruisers had made another turn so that we were now [in] an ideal position for a torpedo attack. The Captain closed the enemy, and when 8,000 yards from the leading battlecruiser turned to port to bring the sights on. Unfortunately at this moment the ship was struck amidships and enveloped in clouds of escaping steam; in the confusion only one of our torpedoes was fired. The Captain sent the Sub-Lieutenant aft to find out what had happened; finding three torpedoes left and sighting [the *Wiesbaden*] a couple of miles away on our beam, [he] aimed and fired a torpedo at her [which] hit below the conning tower. The Sub-Lieutenant then returned to the bridge and reported two torpedoes left, [so] the Captain decided to go in again and [deliver] a final attack on the enemy's battle line which was reappearing out of the mist. [Tovey then] retired at reduced speed [until] two shells exploded in No. 2 boiler-room [and] the ship stopped within range of the enemy. [Fortunately] the battle was surging away from us [and soon] the two fleets were out of sight. At 1915 the *Defender* sighted us: she was also a lame duck having been reduced to ten knots by a 12-inch shell [in] her foremost boiler-room, so our Captain accepted her offer to take us in tow.

But it was 48 hours before 'The Cripple' and 'The Paralytic', as Kipling aptly called them, reached the safety of Aberdeen. With equal gallantry and greater success, the *Acasta*, which had become detached from her flotilla, pressed home a torpedo attack on the *Seydlitz*'s starboard side.

Shortly before 1800 Arbuthnot's First Cruiser Squadron sighted Bödicker's Second Scouting Group returning from their unequal combat with the Third Battlecruiser Squadron. Having no accurate knowledge of Scheer's movements, the Rear-Admiral, who had not forgotten how he had missed his 'golden moment' when Captain of the *Orion* on 10th December 1914, immediately turned in pursuit, opening fire on the crippled *Wiesbaden*. A couple of minutes later Hipper's battlecruisers and Behncke's Third Battle Squadron loomed out of the haze only 7,000 yards away and opened fire at the four British cruisers whose armour had never been intended to withstand heavy shell. 'They were continually hidden by splashes', noted one of the *Neptune*'s officers; 'they were being repeatedly hit and must have been going through hell on earth'.

At first the *Defence* did not appear to be damaged [wrote the Captain of the *Obedient*] but she was being heavily engaged, salvoes dropping all around her. [Then at 1615 a] salvo hit her just abaft the after turret and a big red flame flashed up. The ship heeled to the blow but quickly righted herself and steamed on. Almost immediately [another] salvo [was] seen to strike, this time between the forecastle turret and foremost funnel. [She] was lost to sight in an enormous black cloud which rose to a height of some hundred feet and, quickly clearing, showed no signs of a ship at all.

In that devastating explosion Arbuthnot was lost, together with Captain Ellis and all 900 of his flagship's crew.

The *Warrior* [remembers Captain Molteno] was now between the enemy Battle Fleet and our Fifth Battle Squadron. [So] after giving the *Wiesbaden* two final salvoes from my starboard guns, I withdrew. The *Warspite* was about two miles astern of her squadron, having made a large circle towards the enemy [because] her steering gear had jammed. As she came between the *Warrior* and the enemy battle fleet she drew upon herself all the fire that had previously been concentrated on us, which undoubtedly saved the *Warrior* from being sunk.

She was nonetheless in a sorry state. Hit at least 15 times by heavy projectiles, she had more than 100 killed and wounded. She was on fire aft, her upper deck was a shambles, she had a serious list to starboard and she had suffered such damage to her engine-rooms that all steam was shut off. However, by 1900 she was clear to the west of the battle where she sighted the *Engadine* and ordered her to close. At 2100 Robinson's seaplane-carrier took Molteno's disabled cruiser in tow but (as Flight Lieutenant Rutland recalls)

during the night the weather worsened and [her] stern sank low in the water. At daybreak it was realized that she could not reach port and preparations were made to abandon her. There was a fair sea running, but *Engadine* was a cross-Channel steamer fitted with a huge rubbing strake to facilitate going alongside. Without it we could never have stayed long enough to take off her crew of 900-odd. Our officers and men lined *Engadine*'s side and grabbed each man as he came across. The two ships were working heavily, the noise of rending steel was terrific.

Engadine was holed in several places, and the fenders of hazelwood sticks, wired together, quickly went to pieces. The wounded were passed over on stretchers; the last was being passed when [he] slipped out and fell between the two ships. Several officers and men jumped on bulwarks as though to go down after him, but the Captain shouted that no one was to go over the side. The poor fellow had fetched up on the remains of a fender, but it would be only a matter of seconds before he fell through them, so I went on helping the wounded. Then I saw a group looking over the side; I ran forward and saw that [the man] had drifted far enough ahead to be rescued without any real risk. So I grabbed a rope with a bowline in it, with which two men had been trying to lassoo him, went down the rope, swam to the man, put myself into the bowline and, holding him in my arms, ordered those on deck to heave away.

Unfortunately the man died of his wounds. For his selfless act Rutland added the Albert Medal to the D.S.O. which he gained for his reconnaissance flight at the beginning of the battle. Molteno and his crew gave three cheers as Robinson left the *Warrior* sinking and headed his own ship for Rosyth which was safely reached next day.

The *Black Prince* came to a more fearful end. Also seriously damaged by heavy shell she was forced to withdraw from the action. Because she could still steam at 12 knots, Bonham unwisely decided to follow in the wake of Jellicoe's Battle Fleet. Around midnight his ship was sighted by the *Thüringen* in the middle of Scheer's battle line. Under the concentrated fire of five battleships the *Black Prince* blew up—'a grand but terrible sight' (*Scheer*)—and sank with all her crew. The *Duke of Edinburgh* was the only ship of Arbuthnot's ill-fated squadron to escape destruction; Captain Blackett was able to gain the cover of Jellicoe's Battle Fleet and join up with Heath's cruisers.

The visibility around Windy Corner was such that, although Burney sighted the *Barham* at 1750, Evan-Thomas did not see the *Marlborough* until after 1800. Supposing Burney's flagship to be leading a battle fleet that had already deployed, he tried to take the Fifth Battle Squadron into station ahead of her. When he realized his mistake he rejected the idea of leading across the front of Jellicoe's battleships because this would mask their fire; instead, he made for the rear of the line, an understandable decision but one which made it impracticable for his ships to use their speed in the way the *Grand Fleet Battle Orders* envisaged. This involved the squadron in a large turn to port during which it suffered further punishment from Scheer's battle fleet, and when turning back to starboard the *Warspite*'s helm jammed.

We swung under the *Valiant*'s stern and continued round towards the enemy, getting very close to them [recalls her Executive Officer] until we were on a westerly course when [Captain Phillpotts] managed to steady the ship by working the screws. The whole leading enemy division concentrated on us during this circling and we got heavily hit; everybody thought we had gone. The Huns could not see us for splashes, spray and smoke and ceased firing, luckily for us.*

The *Warspite*'s standby steering engine was accidentally connected with ten degrees of helm on, so that she made a second circle within 10,000 yards of the head of Scheer's line before Phillpotts could regain control of his ship. It was these involuntary turns which saved the *Warrior* from the catastrophe suffered by Arbuthnot's flagship; but the *Warspite* sustained considerable damage from 13 fresh hits, and when her steering gear gave further trouble, Evan-Thomas ordered Phillpotts to drop out of the line and take his ship back to Rosyth, which she reached safely after unsuccessful torpedo attacks by *U51* and *U63*, on 1st June.

All this time Scheer remained in ignorance of the approach of the British battle fleet as it deployed behind the pall of smoke over Windy Corner. In the hope of doing serious damage to a part of the Grand Fleet as a result of Hipper's erroneous report of Hood's battlecruisers as four battleships, the German Commander-in-Chief allowed the head of his line to alter two points to starboard, towards them, before his illusions were abruptly shattered. Over a wide arc ahead the mist was stabbed by bright points of fire from the 24 massive grey ghosts of the mightiest fleet the world has known. At 1817 the *Marlborough* opened fire on the head of Behncke's Squadron; she was followed by the *Agincourt* with all 14 of her 12-inch guns, by the *Revenge* with her eight 15-inch and by many more, of which some engaged Hipper's battlecruisers, others, like the *Iron Duke*, the unfortunate *Wiesbaden*. Jellicoe and all his officers and men had the supreme satisfaction of knowing that at last, after nearly two years of weary waiting, they had brought the High Seas Fleet to battle. Moreover they had surprised Scheer before he could deploy his fleet. Obliged to make the long passage of the swept channel from the Jade to the Horn Reefs with his three battle squadrons in line ahead, he had maintained this formation as he followed Hipper northwards. Jellicoe's battle fleet was now 'crossing his T', seriously endangering the head of the German line of which

* For some days afterwards Scheer believed that his ships had sunk the *Warspite*.

only a few ships were able to reply to the British onslaught; the *Lützow* and *Derfflinger*, the *König, Grosser Kurfürst* and *Markgraf* were all hit whilst Scheer's gunners scored none on their opponents.

Hipper's squadron, on the other hand, gained one more dramatic success against Beatty's. As the *Lion* led her three sisters to the van of the *King George V*,* Hood manœuvred his three ships into station ahead of Beatty's flagship with the skill associated with the name he bore. All seven British battlecruisers were then heavily engaged with Hipper's five, scoring nine hits on the *Lützow* and four on the *Derfflinger* whilst Napier's cruisers executed an unsuccessful torpedo attack. 'It was clear,' says von Hase, 'that the enemy could now see us much better than we could see him. [But at 1829] the veil of mist in front of us split across like the curtain of a theatre. Clear and sharply silhouetted against the horizon we saw the *Invincible* in which, Hood had just hailed her Gunnery Officer in the foretop with the words: 'Your firing is very good. Keep at it as quickly as you can: every shot is telling.' But 'at 1831 the *Derfflinger* fired her last salvo at that ship. For the third time we witnessed the dreadful spectacle that we had already seen in the case of the *Queen Mary* and *Defence*.' A heavy shell struck the *Invincible*'s 'Q' turret and, after an interval of seconds, 'Q' magazine followed by 'P' blew up. Since she was 567 feet long and sank in less than 30 fathoms (180 feet), an officer in the *Indomitable* 'saw [her] two ends standing perpendicularly above water, the ship appearing to have broken in halves, each resting on the bottom. [The] survivors were clinging to floating wreckage; I have never seen anything more splendid than these few cheering as we raced by them.' Just six were rescued by the destroyer *Badger*; the gallant Admiral, Captain Cay and more than 1,000 officers and men lost their lives.

Their sacrifice was not in vain: four of Hipper's ships were now in a worse state than the six surviving British battlecruisers. The *Lützow* was so badly damaged, with a heavy list and her bows deep in the water, that as soon as the German Admiral could extricate his ships by turning SW into the enveloping mist, he called a torpedoboat alongside for himself and his staff, and ordered Harder to make his own way back to harbour with the help of a screen provided by the First Flotilla—without much confidence that she would arrive. Whilst Hartog in the

---

* A manœuvre which Jellicoe facilitated by temporarily reducing his speed to 14 knots, accepting the delay in completing his deployment until 1845 because the smoke from the battlecruisers was fouling the range.

Derfflinger, with the handicap of water streaming through a large gap in his ship's bows and his radio out of action (she had received 20 hits from heavy shell and had 180 killed and wounded), led the remaining four German battlecruisers, Hipper tried to board the *Seydlitz*, only to find von Egidy's ship awash forward up to the middle deck. Since Zenker's crew had been unable to repair any of the *Von der Tann*'s turrets, only the *Moltke* remained fit for action, but it was the best part of two hours before Hipper could board her, rehoist his flag and recover command of his crippled squadron.

Behncke's battleships would have suffered comparable damage if the Germans had not devised a manœuvre which enabled them to escape. A turn away in succession would have invited disaster; a normal turn together was not feasible when the German line was bent round in an arc. Fortunately they had assiduously practised another alternative, *Gefechtkehrtwendung*, in which the rear ship turned first and the others put their helms over in quick succession as each saw her next astern begin to turn. (Since this proved so useful it is of interest to note that Jellicoe was strongly opposed to turning his fleet all ships together. He favoured turns by divisional leaders together, their ships following in succession, even though this had the disadvantage that it might temporarily mask their fire.) Realizing the tactically inferior position in which Jellicoe had caught him, Scheer, with some misgiving because it had never been attempted under fire but nonetheless without hesitation, ordered this 'battle turn' to starboard at 1835. It was so ably executed under cover of smoke made by his torpedoboats that in four minutes the whole German battle fleet was steaming W, directly away from its opponents. Except for the *Lützow* and her escort, which steered a southerly course, Hipper's battlecruisers conformed; so did Bödicker's and Reuter's light cruisers with the result that by 1845 the High Seas Fleet had disappeared into the mist, except for the crippled *Wiesbaden* and the Third Torpedoboat Flotilla. Captain Hollmann had seen that he was in a favourable position to attack, but Commodore Michelson, to his subsequent regret, did not realize this and hoisted Hollmann's recall so as to save his torpedoes for another occasion—though the flotilla managed to fire six at Beatty's battlecruisers before complying.

Nothing exemplifies more the difficulties with which Jellicoe had to contend than the brevity of this first clash between the two battle fleets. Despite the skill with which the British Commander-in-Chief had enmeshed the High Seas Fleet, poor visibility enabled Scheer to extricate his ships from a potentially disastrous position when the *Iron Duke* had fired no more than nine salvoes. Jellicoe had, however, achieved such an enviable position that he had no reason to be despondent, despite his expressed opinion that 'unless the meeting of the fleets take place fairly early in the day, it is most difficult, if not impossible, to fight the action to a finish'. The Grand Fleet was where it could prevent the High Seas Fleet escaping either through the Skagerrak or back to the Jade. Scheer's one compensation was that less than two hours remained before nightfall.

Many of the British vessels, both battleships in the line and cruisers, notably the *Falmouth* and *Canterbury*, observed Scheer's turn, to which the only effective counter was 'a resolute and immediate chase' (*Corbett*), but no captain reported it to his Commander-in-Chief. The *Iron Duke*'s own gunnery control saw it within three minutes but failed to draw their bridge's attention to it. 'At a critical moment in the battle Jellicoe had to rely wholly and solely on his own observations' (*Der Krieg zur See*). And since the poor visibility limited his view to four of Scheer's battleships, he first imagined the enemy's disappearance to be due to the mist thickening. Minutes later (1844) he supposed that Scheer had made a small alteration, when he turned his own battle fleet by divisions to SE. It was another 11 minutes before Jellicoe judged that Scheer must have made a large turn, so altered again, but only as far as S, 90 degrees off the enemy's course. Though he had not hesitated to bring his fleet into action, he was now conforming with his declared policy of not risking his ships by following too closely in the wake of a retiring enemy whom he supposed might launch a massed torpedo-boat attack and sow mines in his path. This erroneous belief was supported at 1855 by an underwater explosion which damaged the *Marlborough*, Captain Ross, flooding a boiler-room and reducing her speed to 17 knots. This was the result of a torpedo, probably a last defiant blow by Reiss's crippled *Wiesbaden*, but Jellicoe did not discount the possibility of a mine. Not for a further ten minutes—30 since Scheer ordered his *Kehrtwendung* to W—did Jellicoe turn his fleet so far as SWbyS. And all this time more ships than Jellicoe's cruisers failed to tell him what had happened to Scheer, while the battlecruisers were delayed in their attempt at pursuit by a gyro compass failure which caused the *Lion* to turn a complete circle (see Appendix III).

None of this was, however, of great importance because Scheer made a decision for which there is no comparable justification. It would have been understandable if he had continued in a westerly direction so as to avoid a further engagement with his superior opponent before nightfall. Instead, at 1852, he ordered Schuur's and Goehle's flotillas to attempt a torpedo attack, and three minutes later reversed his fleet's course by a further *Kehrtwendung*, so that it was again steering straight for Jellicoe's line—back into the snare from which it had just escaped. Some years later the German Commander-in-Chief wrote:

> If the enemy followed us, our action in reversing course [the first time] would be classed as a retreat; if any of our rear ships were damaged we would have to sacrifice them, or be compelled by the enemy to choose an unfavourable course of action. Still less was it feasible to disengage, leaving it to the enemy to decide when he would meet us next morning. The only way to avoid this was to compel the enemy to fight a second engagement by making another determined advance. The success of the first battle turn whilst under fire encouraged me to try this. It would surprise the enemy, upset his plans and, if the blow fell heavily, facilitate a night escape.

The German official historian compared this with the British Fleet's tactics at Trafalgar, quoting Nelson: 'I think it will surprise and confound the enemy; they won't know what I am about'—but conveniently omitted the great Admiral's next sentence: 'It will bring forward a pell-mell battle and that is what I want.' It has also been argued that Scheer was misled by a report from the *Moltke* at 1845 giving the British Battle Fleet's bearing as EbyS; that this information, coupled with his equally erroneous belief that the Third Battlecruiser Squadron comprised four battleships, led him to suppose Jellicoe's line to be further to the south than it was, so that an alteration to E would enable the High Seas Fleet to 'cross the T' of the Grand Fleet's rear. The truth is surely contained in a comment which Scheer made to the Austrian Naval Attaché within a fortnight of the battle: 'I had no definite object. I advanced because I thought I should help the *Wiesbaden* and because the situation was entirely obscure, since I received no W/T [wireless] reports.' Certainly Scheer's cruisers, especially Bödicker's Second Scouting Group which made a half-hearted reconnaissance to the eastward, failed him as badly as Jellicoe's. Scheer also said: 'If I had fought such an action in a peace exercise, I should have lost my command—but it was necessary to escape', which his Chief of Staff, von

Trotha, endorsed by describing his Admiral's decision as 'a model of how not to do it.'

On the British side there was one splendid exception to the cruisers' failure to act as 'the eyes of the fleet'. Goodenough had followed the retiring Scheer, and at 1904 he was able to tell Jellicoe the German Battle Fleet's position and, more important, that it had reversed course. This news, coupled with gunfire to the rear—Gaunt's battleship division driving off Hollmann's Third Flotilla which, after an unsuccessful attempt to rescue the *Wiesbaden*'s crew, fired torpedoes, one narrowly missing the *Neptune*—and the approach of Schuur's and Goehle's flotillas, was enough for Jellicoe to turn his battle fleet back into line ahead steering S at 1909. A minute later Hipper's battlecruisers and Behncke's battle squadron appeared out of the mist to starboard and the British Commander-in-Chief knew that he was again 'crossing his opponent's T'. At 1912 'our fleet presented a marvellously impressive spectacle [to one of the *Neptune*'s midshipmen] as salvo after salvo rolled out along the line'. The unlucky *Wiesbaden* suffered once again —to sink during the coming night with all her crew except for one Chief Stoker. '*Colossus* and *Collingwood* concentrated on the *Lützow*', recalls one of Captain Pound's officers, 'and we fired five salvoes at her, the final range being about 8,400 yards. She burst into flame, listed and turned away', so badly crippled that some hours later her escorting torpedoboats were obliged to hasten her end with a torpedo after rescuing her crew. But most of the British battleships selected targets at the head of Scheer's battle fleet; the *Marlborough* 'sighted three ships of the *König* class and opened fire at [one of them at] a range of 10,750 yards. The sixth, twelfth, thirteenth and fourteenth salvoes were all distinct hits. A large cloud of grey smoke appeared near her foremast.' Beatty's ships, three miles ahead of Jerram's flagship, joined in; at 1920 the *Indomitable* 'reopened fire at the enemy battlecruisers at a range of 14,000 yards, our squadron making splendid practice. Time after time a dull orange glow appeared onboard one or other of their ships. One turned out of the line, her after part enveloped in flame; the remainder emitted dense volumes of smoke which hung above the water like a pall.' The Germans replied to this devastating onslaught to little effect; only one of Jellicoe's battleships was struck. The *Colossus* was 'repeatedly straddled across the forecastle, and a good many splinter holes were made forward from "shorts". One salvo hit us direct at 1916, two shells of approximately 12-inch calibre landing in the fore-super-

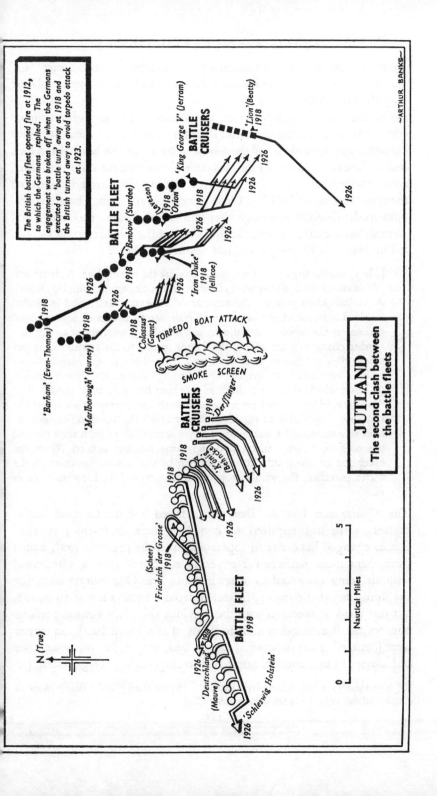

The British battle fleet opened fire at 1912, to which the Germans replied. The engagement was broken off when the Germans executed a 'battle turn' away at 1918 and the British turned away to avoid torpedo attack at 1923.

BATTLE CRUISERS

'Lion' (Beatty)
1918
1926
1926

'King George V' (Jerram)

BATTLE FLEET

'Orion'
1918

'Weyeston'
1918

'Benbow' (Sturdee)
1918

1926

1926

'Iron Duke'
1918 (Jellicoe)

'Colossus'
1918 (Gaunt)

1926

1926

'Barham' (Evan-Thomas)
1918

'Marlborough' (Burney)
1918

1926

1926

TORPEDO BOAT ATTACK

SMOKE SCREEN

BATTLE CRUISERS

'Derfflinger'
1918

'Konig' (Behncke)
1918

1926

1918

~ARTHUR BANKS~

JUTLAND
The second clash between the battle fleets

(Scheer)
'Friedrich der Grosse'
1918

BATTLE FLEET
1918

'Deutschland'
(Mauve)
1926

1918

'Schleswig Holstein'
1926

N (True)

Nautical Miles

0   5

structure, and a third ricocheted on to the armour pad abreast "Q" turret.' But the damage to Pound's ship was slight, only five men being slightly wounded.

On the other hand many of the German dreadnoughts suffered considerably, including their fleet flagship as well as the *König*, in which Behncke was wounded, and the *Grosser Kurfürst* at the head of the line, before Scheer could rectify his mistake and extricate his ships from such a vulnerable position. Deciding to sacrifice his battlecruisers, he signalled them to '*Ran an den Feind*'—'Close the enemy and ram. The ships will fight to the death.'* Although they had already suffered so much, and were without their Admiral, the four ships of the First Scouting Group, led by Hartog's *Derfflinger*, did not hesitate to obey.

> [They] hurled themselves recklessly against the enemy line. A dense hail of fire swept them all the way. Hit after hit struck our ship [the *Derfflinger*]. A 15-inch shell pierced the armour of 'Caesar' turret and exploded inside. Lieutenant-Commander von Boltenstern had both legs torn off and nearly the whole gunhouse crew was killed. The shell set on fire two cordite charges [from which] the flames spread to the transfer chamber where they set fire to four more and from there to the case-chamber where four more were ignited. The burning cases emitted great tongues of flame which shot up as high as a house; but they only blazed, they did not explode as had been the case with the enemy. This saved the ship, but killed [all but five] of the 70 men inside the turret. A few minutes later this catastrophe was followed by a second. A 15-inch shell pierced the roof of 'Dora' turret and the same horrors ensued. With the exception of one man who was thrown by the concussion through the turret entrance, the whole crew of 80 men were killed instantly. (*Von Hase*)

The *Seydlitz* and *Von der Tann* also suffered but the German battle-cruisers were not required to complete their death-ride; at 1917 Scheer changed his order to 'operate against the enemy's van', which gave them more latitude for covering his Battle Fleet's withdrawal without being subjected to overwhelming fire. One minute later, for the third time that evening, Scheer ordered a battle turn of 16 points, but this was not executed with the previous skill; 'for several perilous minutes the fleet flagship and the ships of the Third Battle Squadron were [compelled to] proceed at slow speed, very close to one another and almost in line abreast. Some had to stop engines or go astern [so

---

* Von Hase's version. A literal translation is: 'At the enemy, stake all. Ships are to attack without regard for the consequences.'

19 *German battlecruisers in the North Sea*

20 *British dreadnoughts: in foreground H.M.S.* Agincourt, *armed with fourteen 12-inch g behind her H.M.S.* Erin, *armed with ten 13·5-inch guns*

21 *The finest fleet the world has seen: British battle squadrons in the North Sea*

that] they lay with little way on, bunched together, and forming an admirable target for the enemy's guns' (*Der Krieg zur See*). Behncke's flagship helped to save the situation by hauling out to windward and making a smoke screen, the *Friedrich der Grosse* made her turn to port and Captain Natzmer hastened the manœuvre by putting the *Ostfries-land*'s helm over without waiting for the *Thüringen*. The crisis was over by 1935 when Scheer's battleships were again heading west at the maximum speed of Mauve's pre-dreadnoughts, followed by the four German battlecruisers which, almost miraculously, had survived their sacrificial ordeal. After being subjected to the devastating salvoes of Jellicoe's battle fleet for just 15 minutes, as compared with some 25 on the first occasion, the German heavy ships disappeared into the mist and the British were compelled to cease fire, when, to take a typical example, the *Agincourt* had discharged no more than ten salvoes from her 14 big guns.

Observing the confusion into which Scheer's fleet had been thrown, why did Jellicoe allow his opponent to elude him in this way for a second time? Scheer had ordered his flotillas to make an attack to cover his turn, but only Schultz's and Goehle's, which had the advantage of having been instructed to do this some 20 minutes before, were able to comply. The Third, Fifth and Seventh Flotillas were too far to the northward and Schuur's boats were so slow in moving out that they had to be recalled. The Sixth and Ninth Flotillas were engaged by the British battleships' secondary armaments and counter-attacked by Le Mesurier's light cruisers and Hawksley's Eleventh Destroyer Flotilla; nonetheless, despite losses among their 20 boats, they closed to under 8,000 yards and fired 31 torpedoes. Only ten of these reached the British line, but their effect was out of all proportion; with justification, since Beatty gained the same impression, Jellicoe believed his battle fleet to be threatened by a massed flotilla attack. In the Russo-Japanese war less than five per cent of more than 100 torpedoes fired had hit their targets, yet enthusiastic British (and German) protagonists of this new weapon had convinced their admirals that more than 30 per cent of the faster, longer-range torpedoes available by 1914 would hit unless drastic avoiding action was taken. Jellicoe's orders not only emphasized the need for this, but stressed that the best countermeasure was to turn away by divisions, whereby the ships might outrun the torpedoes' range. And nothing prior to Jutland had shown that, in poor visibility, this would have a greater disadvantage than temporarily increasing gun range by 3–4,000 yards—that of losing contact with the enemy, so that in such conditions the more risky alternative of turning towards might be justified. ('I did not agree with the whole line having to turn away from a torpedo threat; a turn towards in some cases might be more efficacious' [*Sturdee*]; 'I fancy that a turn towards might some-times be a useful counter' [*Jellicoe's comment written in 1936*]; see also p. 113). At 1923, coincident with Scheer's third battle turn, Jellicoe ordered his fleet to turn away. He was so reluctant to do this that he limited the alteration to two points, but a couple of minutes later was persuaded to make it two more. Thus, as the German Battle Fleet swung round to W, the Grand Fleet turned to SE which hastened the moment when Scheer's ships disappeared without altogether avoiding the torpedo danger. Several of Jellicoe's battleships had to comb the tracks: the *Marlborough*, for example, 'altered course to star-board so that [one] track passed ahead, number two passed so close astern that we should certainly have been hit if the stern had not been swinging under helm, [whilst] number three must have been running below depth [because it] went right under the ship'.

However, Jellicoe's decision to turn away from Scheer at this junc-ture was not of itself the reason why he lost contact with an opponent reluctant to face a superior fleet. The British Commander-in-Chief again thought that the enemy's 'temporary disappearance was due to a thickening of the mist [and] no report of this movement of the German Fleet reached me', although Scheer's turn was clearly seen by several battleships at the rear of his line, notably the *Valiant* as early as 1923. When he judged the torpedo threat to be over at 1935, he supposed an alteration of five points—one more than his turn away—would be sufficient to return within gun range. Since Scheer, after first steering W, had altered to the three-point diverging course of SW, the result was, to quote the *Malaya*'s report, that 'this was the last seen of the enemy in daylight' by most of the British battleships.

Even Goodenough, who saw that Scheer was on this course, failed to report it. However, at 1940 Jellicoe realized from a signal made by the *Lion* that his turn had not been enough and altered again, but only so far as a course parallel to his unseen opponent. Meantime Beatty's inherent determination to 'engage the enemy more closely' was not again spoiled by compass trouble. Moving out to starboard he was in action with the German battlecruisers, and at 1945 was able to report the bearing of the head of Scheer's battle fleet, and, more important,

its course. Unfortunately Goodenough confused the issue by an erroneous report that an unknown number of enemy ships had been detached to the NW. Not until 2000, when Scheer was some 15 miles
away, did Jellicoe take the drastic action needed to regain contact with
his opponent, in the hour left before darkness, by turning his Battle
Fleet to W, though he did not increase speed to more than the damaged
Marlborough's maximum of 17 knots. One minute later the British
Commander-in-Chief received a signal from Beatty, originated at
1947: 'Submit van of battleships follow battlecruisers. We can then
cut off whole of enemy's battle fleet', towards which he had sent his
light cruisers to keep in touch. But to the transit delay suffered by this
message Jellicoe added another: he waited nearly 15 minutes before
ordering Jerram to 'follow our battlecruisers'—with no sense of
urgency and without indicating why—by which time Beatty's ships had
not only lost contact but were no longer in sight from the *King George V*.
So, without increasing speed, Jerram steered for the direction in which
he had last seen Beatty, and from which he had just heard a burst of
gunfire (from Napier's cruisers), without knowing that he had turned
two points *away* from the enemy.

Nonetheless, the two fleets were still converging because Scheer was
so concerned at the way he was being headed away from his base—
every four miles he was forced to the westward added another half-
hour to his journey—that he had altered to S at 1945 when the *Iron
Duke* was only about 12 miles to the east. 'The reports made by my
flotillas made it certain we had been in action with the whole British
Fleet', he wrote. 'Should we succeed in checking the enemy's enveloping movement and reaching the Horn Reefs before them, we should
retain the initiative for next morning. With this object, all flotillas had to
be used for attacks during the night, at the risk of having to do without
them in the new engagements which might be expected at dawn. The
Battle Fleet had to make for the Horn Reefs by the shortest route,
maintaining this course against all attacks made by the enemy.' One
result of this was the last contacts between the two fleets before nightfall.

At 2020 the enemy battlecruisers were again sighted [noted one of the
Indomitable's officers] and a few seconds later they opened fire. Most of my
turret's crew had come up for a breath of fresh air, so they tumbled
back in a hurry and by 2026 we were hard at it again at a range of
8,800 yards. The German firing was fairly good and we were straddled

several times. Many of our squadron's salvoes hit and large fires were observed onboard several of their ships. By 2042 they had had enough and drew off, so we ceased firing. Should it be my good fortune to be engaged in another action, I shall take care that only one gramophone is taken into the turret. We had one in the gunhouse and one in the working chamber [just below] and during every lull these two were playing simultaneously, each with a different record. The result was one of the real horrors of the war.

The German battlecruisers, which were trying to get into station ahead of Scheer's Battle Fleet, were 'subjected to a heavy fire [from Beatty's force but] only the flashes of the enemy's salvoes could be seen. The ships which were already seriously damaged received further hits without being able to make any serious reply.' Only two of the *Derfflinger*'s 12-inch guns remained in action and she was flooded with more than 3,000 tons of water. 'They therefore turned away and took up a position on the disengaged side' (*Scheer*). This contact occurred just as Hipper was trying to board the *Moltke*, and was one reason why he had to defer regaining control of his squadron until after 2100.

Napier's cruisers were also engaged; according to one of the *Yarmouth*'s officers,

> we were ordered to sweep to the westward to locate the head of the enemy's line and were in the process of spreading from the *Falmouth* when at 2020 five enemy light cruisers were observed bearing NNW. They were followed by two battlecruisers which were being engaged by our battlecruisers. We formed single line and engaged the enemy light cruisers at about 7,000 yards. Their salvoes were all short, and ours may have been as bad for it was impossible to spot under the almost hopeless conditions of light. The enemy drew off and we never saw them again.

Next, Beatty's ships sighted Mauve's pre-dreadnoughts on which they turned their guns. Hits on the *Schleswig-Holstein*, *Pommern* and *Hessen* were enough to turn this squadron, which was now leading the German battle fleet, away to the SW where it disappeared from view. Le Mesurier and Hawksley also saw them but—and there is no more revealing statement of the way in which so many of the British cruiser captains failed their Commander-in-Chief—'observing that the *King George V* had altered course away from us, we deemed it necessary *to follow her so as not to lose touch* [with our own fleet]'.* No wonder Beatty

* Author's italics.

added the following to his fighting instructions after the battle: 'It becomes the duty of subordinate leaders to anticipate executive orders and act in the spirit of the Commander-in-Chief's requirements. There are only two and they are very simple: so long as the enemy heavy ships remain afloat we must locate and report, attack and destroy.'

A little earlier, at 2010, Hawksley saw Heinecke's Fifth Flotilla, which was to the east of the rest of Scheer's fleet, and led his destroyers in an attack on them, supported by the Fourth Light Cruiser Squadron. The British ships thus sighted Behncke's Squadron, now at the rear of Scheer's line. Hawksley missed his opportunity for a torpedo attack, but Le Mesurier's ships did better. One of the *Calliope*'s officers wrote that

> we turned on to a course parallel to [the enemy] after closing to about 8,500 yards to fire a torpedo. We were not fired at previous to turning, possibly because they could not make us out as friend or enemy, but they proceeded to rectify the error as soon as we turned and got our range quickly. Having fired our torpedo, we proceeded at full speed on an easterly course to join our own [fleet]. We were in sight of the German battleships for perhaps ten minutes [and] were hit five times in all. Only our high speed and zigzagging saved us from annihilation.

The damage to Le Mesurier's flagship prevented him signalling a report, but Jellicoe saw something of this engagement for himself and at 2038 flashed to the *Comus*: 'What are you firing at?' The reply, 'Enemy battle fleet', suggested that the Admiral was achieving his purpose, closing the enemy. This seemed to be confirmed a moment later when firing broke out towards the British rear: Goodenough's squadron had encountered the German Second Flotilla.

> Whilst it was still twilight [recalls one of the *Nottingham*'s officers] we had a short action with German [torpedoboats] of which the *Southampton* claimed to have sunk one; but they disappeared in the mist and failing light before we could come to decisive range. Personally I had been on the bridge since 1400 with no extra clothing on and I don't think I had ever felt so cold before, but one cannot send people down to one's cabin to fetch an overcoat in the middle of the Battle of Jutland.

Jellicoe had to wait until 2100 for full reports from the *Lion* and the *Falmouth* before the situation was reasonably clear to him. A third, more crucial encounter followed. The light cruisers *Caroline* and *Royalist*, stationed ahead of the *King George V* in which Jerram had for three quarters of an hour been trying to follow Beatty's unseen ships 'to cut off whole of enemy battle fleet', sighted Scheer's line. Captains Crooke and Meade immediately turned to attack Mauve's pre-dread-noughts with torpedoes as they reported this to Jerram. Largely because 'his Navigating Officer, who had just come from the Battle-cruiser Fleet, was certain that the ships sighted were our battlecruisers', Jerram negatived the attack. When Crooke repeated that they were the enemy, Jerram answered, 'If you are quite sure, attack', whereupon the *Caroline* and *Royalist* fired their torpedoes. Hawksley also sighted these ships, identified them as enemy and turned towards, expecting Jerram's squadron to open fire. But they did not do so; as he freely acknowledged afterwards, the Admiral remained convinced that they were Beatty's ships. Not everyone in the Second Battle Squadron shared this view; Leveson's Flag Lieutenant in the *Orion* said: 'Sir, if you leave the line now and turn towards, your name will be as famous as Nelson's'. But like Evan-Thomas, Leveson had been schooled to obey; after a moment's hesitation he answered: 'We must follow the next ahead.' As Scheer's ships hurriedly turned again to the west before resuming their southerly course, Jerram continued to lead the British battle fleet on a parallel course instead of a closing one.

This was the last meeting between units of the two great fleets before night finally closed over the North Sea little more than 50 miles from the Danish coast—but the sun would rise on a new day in five hours' time. Despite serious losses for which much of the credit must go to Hipper and his battlecruisers, the Grand Fleet, under Jellicoe's cool, steadfast direction, remained in command of the situation. Scheer had twice fled from the thunderous cannonade of his opponent's heavy guns, and the Grand Fleet stretched in a line more than ten miles long between the High Seas Fleet and the safety of its harbours. There had been no Trafalgar on 31st May, in large measure because contact had been made so late in the day, because Scheer was intent on avoiding action and because of the mist—but British officers and men had high hopes of another 'Glorious First of June'.

5

Night

'The German Battle Fleet, aided by low visibility, avoided prolonged action with our main forces, and soon after these appeared on the scene returned to port.'

Admiralty communiqué of 2nd June 1916

'Violent action flared up in the darkness to the NW, passed astern across our wake and died away towards the east. Something tremendous was going on only a few miles away, but to our astonishment (it surprises me still) the Battle Fleet continued to steam to the southward.'

An officer of H.M.S. 'Canada' (now Rear-Admiral Sir William Jameson), in 1961

SCHEER was so determined to reach the swept channel through the minefields to the south of the Horn Reefs before dawn* in order to save his fleet from annihilation next day, that he accepted the chances of a night action which he believed would cost him less. The German ships were equipped and trained for night fighting; not so the British, whose policy was to avoid an engagement during the dark hours: they had an inadequate number of searchlights with indifferent control arrangements, and they had not been provided with starshell with which the enemy could be illuminated without providing his guns with a point of aim. Indeed, these were such a novelty to the British Fleet that one captain wrote: 'The enemy was making use of white fireballs for some purpose or another.' Consequently Jellicoe 'rejected the idea of a night action as leading to possible disaster, first owing to the presence of torpedo craft in large numbers and, secondly, to the impossibility of distinguishing between our own and enemy vessels'.

* Sunrise was shortly after 0200.

But this was not all; he thought it unlikely that his opponent, after twice turning so sharply away from the British Battle Fleet, would risk running into it during the night by making for the Horn Reefs when two other swept routes to the Jade were available. He 'decided to steer to the southward where I should be in a position to renew the engagement at daylight and should be favourably placed to intercept the enemy should he make for Heligoland or towards the Ems and thence along the north German coast'.

Accordingly the British Commander-in-Chief closed up his battle fleet at 2117 into its night cruising order of four columns in line ahead disposed abeam. Jerram's Second Battle Squadron was nearest the enemy; next to the east came Sturdee's Fourth, led by the *Iron Duke*; then Burney's First, whilst Evan-Thomas's three 'Queen Elizabeths' occupied the port wing. Jellicoe signalled no 'night intentions'*; his battleship captains were left to assume that they could expect a relatively quiet night followed by a renewal of the action next day. Beatty shared his Commander-in-Chief's appreciation:

> I continued on a south-westerly course until 2124. Nothing further being sighted I assumed the enemy to be to the NW and that we had established ourselves well between him and his base. [On receiving Jellicoe's signal] that the course of the Fleet was S, in view of the damaged condition of [my] battlecruisers, and our strategic position being such as to make it appear certain that we should locate the enemy at daylight under most favourable circumstances, I did not consider it desirable or proper to close [him] during the dark hours. I concluded that I should be carrying out the Commander-in-Chief's wishes by turning to the course of the Fleet, my duty [being] to ensure that the enemy fleet could not regain its base by passing round the southern flank of our forces.

Accordingly Beatty led his ships to a station 15 miles WSW of the *Iron Duke*. Alexander-Sinclair's and Napier's light cruisers went with them; Goodenough's had already taken station astern of Burney's battle squadron whilst Heath's and Le Mesurier's had gone to the east of Evan-Thomas's, although this was the side away from the enemy.

Jellicoe did not ignore the possibility that Scheer would attempt the

* In common with most flag officers of his time Jellicoe was accustomed to initiate all his own signals. He did not realize that in battle more comprehensive ones than brief orders for courses and speeds, deployment and stationing, opening and ceasing fire might be needed, whose drafting must be delegated to staff officers.

Horn Reefs route. At 2127 he ordered his destroyer flotillas to follow five miles astern of his battle fleet.

> If I put [them there] they would fulfil three conditions. They would be in an excellent position for attacking the enemy *should* [he] *turn with a view to regaining* [his] *base during the night.** They would be in a position to attack enemy [torpedoboats] should the latter search for our fleet with a view to a night attack on [our] heavy ships. Finally, they would be clear of our own ships, and the danger of them attacking our battleships in error, or of our battleships firing on them, would be reduced to a minimum.

He overlooked two points; that by this time his destroyers had little idea of the whereabouts of the enemy, not to mention their own battle-cruisers and cruiser squadrons, and that Hawksley, though recently appointed Commodore Grand Fleet Flotillas, had had insufficient time to train them in co-ordinated attacks, least of all during the night. Both were serious handicaps: the British destroyers were not only as much in the dark metaphorically as they were in reality but, if a possible enemy should be sighted, each flotilla had to act on its own—and the torpedo was such an imprecise weapon that only massed attacks could be expected to achieve significant results. Jellicoe also detached the *Abdiel* at 2205 to lay her mines off the Horn Reefs Light, which she proceeded to do without incident by 0200, subsequently returning to Rosyth.

Such news as the British Commander-in-Chief gleaned from his ships around this time, notably Jerram's rejection of the *Caroline*'s report, and one from Beatty at 2138 giving the enemy's course as WSW, led him to suppose that the High Seas Fleet was well to the NW. In reality it was only eight miles away because Scheer had altered to a little east of SSE at 2114, since when he had been converging on Jellicoe at an acute angle at a speed restricted by Mauve's squadron to 16 knots. This course 'is to be maintained', he told his captains, because it led straight for the Horn Reefs where, in a signal sent at 2106, he asked for a morning zeppelin reconnaissance. So that his battleships, whose sequence had been reversed by their last 'battle turn', should be led by the undamaged First Squadron, headed by the *Westfalen*, Captain Red-lich, Scheer ordered his pre-dreadnoughts to the rear. Mauve was about to comply when the *Schleswig-Holstein*, Captain Barrentrapp, reported a white light to port which was identified as coming from the masthead of a

* Author's italics.

British cruiser. The offending vessel was one of Goodenough's which saw nothing of their bigger opponents. Nor, a few minutes later, did Beatty's battlecruisers sight the cruisers of the Second and Fourth Scouting Groups, which were both on the side of their Battle Fleet nearest the enemy where they were so fortunate as to see the *Lion* flash to the *Princess Royal*: 'Please give me challenge and reply now in force as they have been lost'. The *Lion*'s need for these is understandable, but the use of so bright a light, which gave the High Seas Fleet the current British recognition signals, was to have considerable consequences. All three German Commanders decided against revealing themselves by opening fire, whilst Mauve waited until the Second Light Cruiser Squadron had disappeared before turning his ships. Scheer's Battle Fleet did not, therefore, attain its night disposition until 2200, by which time Hipper's much-battered battlecruisers had been ordered to the rear.

Nearly two hours earlier Scheer had decided on an offensive move to assist his fleet's escape: Michelson (in the *Rostock*) was to conduct night attacks with all available torpedoboats. But though the Germans were trained in such tactics, the need for a searching force to locate the enemy before commencing an attack had not been understood. Moreover, Michelson soon found that Heinrich (in the *Regensburg*) had forestalled Scheer's order: selecting those boats which had more than one torpedo left—Schuur's Second and three of Schultz's Sixth—he had ordered them to execute an attack at 2045* in the sector ENE to ESE where he believed the British Battle Fleet to be, whilst the rest of Schultz's boats and Goehle's Ninth Flotilla went to screen Scheer's battle squadrons or to join Michelson. The latter decided to allow his colleagues' arrangements to stand and ordered his own good flotillas, Heinecke's Fifth and Koch's Seventh, to start attacks at 2100 in two sectors more to the south, believing that one, at least, would find the British Battle Fleet.

The Second Flotilla approached too soon: there was still enough light for it to be counter-attacked and driven off by Goodenough's cruisers and Hawksley's Eleventh Flotilla before it could get within range. Half an hour later Heinrich tried again, only to find that he was

---

* In a comprehensive signal which highlights the better standard of staff work in the German Fleet.

too far astern of the British Battle Fleet to achieve anything. Joined by Hollmann's Third Flotilla (which had become detached from Michelson's group), he set course for the Skaw by which route some 20 torpedo-boats reached Kiel next day, having taken no further part in the battle.

Michelson's attacks suffered other handicaps. Soon after 2130 Koch's boats were fired on by Behncke's battleships, fortunately without serious consequences. More important, for fear that funnel sparks from dirty fires would disclose their approach, both flotillas limited their speed to 18 knots so that they made contact with Jellicoe's destroyers instead of with his battle fleet. At 2150 Koch sighted Wintour's Fourth Flotilla steering N towards its station for the night. Supposing it to be screening Jellicoe's heavy ships, the Germans fired four torpedoes without result; at the crucial moment the Fourth Flotilla happened to turn to the British fleet's course of S. One vessel, H.M.S. *Garland*, Lieutenant-Commander R. S. Goff, saw the enemy and opened fire, but Wintour decided against pursuit. This allowed Koch to attempt another attack, but by this time his boats were too far to the rear; like Heinrich's, they passed well astern of the Grand Fleet, then steered for the Horn Reefs. Thereafter, to quote von Hase, 'it is much to be regretted that throughout the whole night our destroyers searching for the great British Fleet failed to find it, although they knew exactly where it was last seen'.

At about 2140 the *Frankfurt* and *Pillau* sighted the *Castor* and the Eleventh Destroyer Flotilla, likewise moving to their station for the night. But the visibility was so treacherous that the British vessels saw nothing of the Second Scouting Group as it fired torpedoes at six cables, then altered away without opening fire or burning searchlights, 'so as to avoid drawing the [British] destroyers after them towards [the German] Battle Fleet' (*Der Krieg zur See*). Half an hour later the Second Scouting Group closed the *Castor*'s flotilla again. This time Hawksley saw their shadowy shapes on his starboard bow but supposed them to be friendly ships because they flashed the current British challenge. The four German cruisers closed to little more than a mile before switching on searchlights and opening a murderous fire from which the *Castor* suffered considerable damage, most of it above the upper deck, and numerous casualties among her more exposed personnel before she could reply. 'Of the eight destroyers astern of [her] two fired torpedoes [of which one passed under the *Elbing*], but some were so blinded by the *Castor*'s guns that they could see nothing, and others were so certain that a mistake had been made, and that they were being fired on by our own ships, that they decided not to fire their torpedoes' (*Hawksley*). The advantage gained by the Germans in this brief engagement, in which only one of their ships, the *Hamburg,* suffered appreciable damage, was as much due to Jellicoe's failure to give his destroyers adequate information about the enemy and his own fleet at nightfall as to Bödicker's clever use of the signals he had intercepted between the *Lion* and *Princess Royal.** Like Wintour, Hawksley did not attempt to maintain contact; because the *Grand Fleet Battle Orders* did not envisage using destroyers for night attacks, and because Jellicoe had signalled no other instructions, the Commodore believed it to be his prime duty to keep in touch with his own Battle Fleet so as to be available for action next morning.†

This engagement was quickly followed by one between Goodenough's and Reuter's squadrons.

> At about 2215 [recalls Lieutenant King-Hall] there appeared on our starboard beam, scarcely 1,500 yards distant, a line of five ships steering in the same direction. The next few minutes were full of suspense, the newcomers being as unwilling to disclose their identity as we were. Then the two squadrons almost simultaneously decided that the other was hostile and opened a violent fire. The action lasted three-and-a-half minutes. The four leading German ships concentrated their lights and guns on the *Southampton,* the fifth fired at the *Dublin.* The *Nottingham* and *Birmingham,* with great wisdom, did not switch on their lights and were not fired at. The range was amazingly close. There could be no missing. A gun was fired and a hit obtained; the gun was loaded, it flamed, it roared, it leapt to the rear, it slid to the front; there was another hit. But to load guns there must be men; flesh and blood must lift the shells and cordite, and open and close the hungry breeches. But flesh and blood cannot stand high explosives and there was a great deal of high explosive bursting along H.M.S. *Southampton*'s upper deck. It is after the firing that the real horror of a night action begins. We did not know where the Germans were, our guns' crews were practically non-existent, the voicepipes and telephones were in shreds. We simply had to have time to reorganize, so we didn't dare show a light. Yet the upper deck was strewn with dead and wounded.

* The Grand Fleet, whose recognition signals took the form of morse code letters made with an ordinary *white* light, was never able to simulate those used by the High Seas Fleet because the German Navy had wisely developed a system requiring special *coloured* lights.

† Orders for all available destroyers to form a night attacking force were not added to the *Grand Fleet Battle Orders* until October 1916.

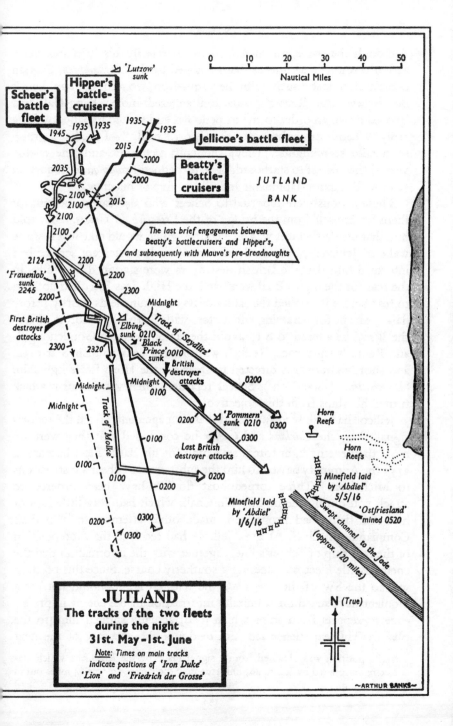

JUTLAND

The tracks of the two fleets
during the night
31st. May - Ist. June

Note: Times on main tracks
indicate positions of 'Iron Duke'
'Lion' and 'Friedrich der Grosse'

Although the damage inflicted on the *Dublin* in this brief but fierce action was not so serious as that sustained by the *Southampton*, Captain Scott's ship lost touch with her squadron; so did Captain Duff's *Birmingham*. But Reuter's squadron suffered more; King-Hall had 'passed down an order to the torpedo flat and waited impatiently for a reply. When it came through—the report "ready"—I fired at a group of hostile searchlights. [They] suddenly went out and [the enemy vessel] sheered off to starboard.' The torpedoed *Frauenlob* subsequently sank with Captain Hoffmann and all but five of his crew.

These actions were reported to Scheer who also saw something of them for himself from the bridge of the *Friedrich der Grosse*. They told him that his Battle Fleet was on a course which would take it across the wake of Jellicoe's, because the German wireless intercept service had informed him that the British destroyers were stationed five miles in the rear for the night. If all went well, the High Seas Fleet had nothing to fear before it reached the safety of its own minefields shortly before dawn, except for harassing encounters with British light forces. When the *Westfalen* altered to S to avoid the action between Goodenough's and Reuter's squadrons, Redlich was ordered back to SEbyS at 2234, and shortly afterwards directed to steer for the Horn Reefs lightship. '*Durchalten!*' ('Stand on'), Scheer repeated whenever a British attack turned his ships from this objective.

Jellicoe had also seen and heard these engagements; from the reports signalled by the *Garland* and *Castor* he concluded that they were no more than enemy light forces searching for his Battle Fleet because at 2155 the Admiralty passed to him the substance of Scheer's instructions to Michelson: 'Three torpedoboat flotillas have been ordered to attack you during the night'. Whitehall, which had very little idea of how the battle had progressed, made other attempts to help their Commander-in-Chief. At 2123 Jellicoe had received the 2100 position of the rear ship of Scheer's line, together with the information that the enemy Battle Fleet was steering a southerly course. Since this position was to the SW of the *Iron Duke*, he rejected it: 'I should not for a moment have relied on Admiralty information of the enemy in preference to reports from ships which [had] actually sighted him [to the NW].'* This experience led him to doubt the accuracy of the next

---

* The position was obtained from a signal made by the *Regensburg* which was correctly deciphered by Room 40; unfortunately the *Regensburg* was 14 miles out in her reckoning.

intelligence which he received from the Admiralty. Between 2155 and 2210 Room 40 produced the deciphered texts of four messages from Scheer. The War Room combined three of these into a signal which Jellicoe received at 2330: 'German Battle Fleet ordered home at 2114. Battlecruisers in rear. Course SSE¾E. Speed 16 knots.' Whilst most of this agreed with the British Admiral's appreciation, he rejected the course because it meant that the German Battle Fleet must be very near his rear when two recent reports from his own ships—Goodenough's of his action with the Fourth Scouting Group (delayed by the need to pass it through the *Nottingham* because the *Southampton*'s wireless had been wrecked) and one from the *Birmingham* of a later momentary sighting of Hipper's battlecruisers—had confirmed his belief that the High Seas Fleet was remaining to the north-westward. (Duff's report was, by an unlucky chance, unintentionally misleading; shortly after 2315, for reasons to be related, the High Seas Fleet was obliged to alter away to WbyS before turning back to S—when Duff made his sighting—and then resuming its south-easterly course for the Horn Reefs.) However, this should have been of small importance because the fourth message intercepted by Room 40 was Scheer's request for a zeppelin reconnaissance. This gave the clearest indication of the way the High Seas Fleet was returning home. Yet it was not passed to Jellicoe. The charitable explanation is that 'the Chief of Staff had left the War Room to snatch some much needed rest and had left in charge an officer who had no experience of German operational signals and was unaware of the significance of this signal' (*Admiral James*). The truth lies in Thomas Jackson's already mentioned distrust of the work of Room 40. (For security reasons no other officer in the Operations Division was allowed access to the 'special intelligence' produced by Room 40.) 'Of course, if the Admiralty had given me the information as to the airship reconnaissance at the Horn Reefs I should have altered in that direction during the night', Jellicoe wrote afterwards. As it was, the British Fleet held its course whilst the Admiral, reasonably assured that he could expect to achieve a decisive victory by a day-long gunnery duel with the enemy's heavy ships beginning soon after dawn, retired to his shelter at the back of the *Iron Duke*'s bridge to take what rest he could during the three hours of darkness that remained.

These hours did not pass without Jellicoe's rest being disturbed. More signals, bursts of gunfire and the white glare of searchlight beams were reported to him; but not all was reported that should have been, either by the Admiralty or by his own admirals and captains. He did not know that Bödicker's three remaining ships clashed with the most westerly of the British flotillas, Wintour's Fourth; to quote an officer from the *Spitfire*, commanded by Lieutenant-Commander C. W. Trelawney:

> The night was dark, and we had absolutely no idea of where the enemy were, and only a very vague idea of the position of our own ships. The flotilla was in line ahead, Captain 'D' [Wintour] in the *Tipperary* leading, followed by *Spitfire*, *Sparrowhawk* and some eight other destroyers with *Broke* in the middle. About [2315] we could distinguish three cruisers steaming at high speed on our starboard quarter, closing in about 20 degrees to our course. We concluded that they must be British but when they were in to 500 to 700 yards range *Tipperary* made the challenge. In reply all three ships [the *Frankfurt, Pillau* and *Elbing*] switched on a blaze of searchlights, the majority trained on the *Tipperary*; only a few stray beams lit us and our next astern. After a short pause a rain of shell was concentrated on our unfortunate leader and in less than a minute she was hit and badly on fire forward.

One of the *Tipperary*'s officers tells how, 'the enemy's second salvo hit and burst one of our main steam pipes [so that] the turbines were brought to a standstill and we dropped out of the action. Aft we had been hit by only three shells and only a few men were wounded, but the majority stationed amidships were killed or wounded, while forward [where] the ship was on fire, [there were] only two survivors', who did not include Captain Wintour.

Meanwhile, the *Spitfire*, followed by the two boats astern of her, and the *Broke*, Commander W. L. Allen, had turned and fired torpedoes. 'Much to our joy [one] was seen to get the second enemy ship between the after funnels and the mainmast and she seemed to stop firing, heel over and all her lights went out.' The smitten ship was the *Elbing* which some nine hours earlier had fired the first shot in the battle. Recoiling from this attack, Madlung, together with his two squadron mates, tried to escape by steering through the head of Scheer's battle fleet. Captains Trotha and Mommsen were successful in reaching the protective lee of Schmidt's First Battle Squadron,* but Madlung's stricken vessel lacked the necessary power of manœuvre: she was ram-

---

* Both captains were, apparently, so affected by this encounter that when later they ran into Stirling's Twelfth Flotilla they thought it best to take no action but to make good their escape.

med by Rear-Admiral Engelhardt's flagship, the dreadnought *Posen*, Captain Lange, and this second blow flooded the *Elbing*'s engine-rooms, depriving her of all steam.

After Bödicker's retirement, the leading ships of the Fourth Flotilla came under heavy fire from the *Westfalen*, *Nassau* and *Rheinland*, at the head of Scheer's line. The British vessels put up a spirited fight, their 4-inch guns doing appreciable damage to the upper works of their massive opponents. Mercifully, the German shooting at such close range was poor: although the *Westfalen* fired nearly 150 rounds from her 5·9-inch and smaller calibre guns in four minutes, only one destroyer suffered seriously. Trelawney, having discovered that the *Spitfire* could fire no more torpedoes,

> decided to return to the *Tipperary*, now a mass of burning wreckage. As we neared [her] we saw [the *Nassau*, Captain Klappenbach] trying to ram us, coming at full speed across our port bow. The Captain ordered, 'Hard-a-starboard; full speed ahead both', and shouted, 'Clear the forecastle'. It wasn't a minute too soon; the two ships met bow to bow I recollect a fearful crash, then being hurled across the deck and feeling the *Spitfire* rolling over to starboard as no sea ever made her roll. As we bumped the enemy opened fire with their [11-inch] guns, though luckily they could not depress them to hit us, but the blast cleared everything before it. Our foremast came tumbling down, our forward searchlight found its way from above the bridge down to the deck and the foremost funnel was blown back like the hinged funnel of a river steamboat. The enemy surged down our port side clearing everything before her; the boats came crashing down, the davits [being] torn out of their sockets. But none of her shells hit us except for two which passed through the canvas screens round the bridge, [where] with the exception of the Captain [who suffered a head wound], the Coxswain and one seaman, everyone was killed. Eventually the [*Nassau*] cleared us astern and disappeared, leaving us still afloat but drifting in a somewhat pitiful condition. The damage to [our] bows and ship's side was considerable; about 60 odd feet from our stem aft along the port side had been torn away and in exchange the enemy had left 20 feet of her upper deck inside our messdeck. [However,] the engineers decided that the good ship was capable of steaming with three out of the four boilers, and the bulkheads were holding all right, so the after steering position was connected up [and] we shaped course W, speed six knots.

In this way 'with the remains of a chart patched together', the *Spitfire* began her journey home through a rising wind and sea. She made a landfall some 36 hours later and steamed into the Tyne in the afternoon of 2nd June.

The brunt of this clash was borne by the leading British destroyers because those to the rear were almost certain that Bödicker's ships were British cruisers making a disastrous mistake, until stray searchlight beams chanced to illuminate the unmistakable shapes of 'Helgoland' class dreadnoughts. The close proximity of at least part of Scheer's Battle Fleet was then revealed to Allen of the *Broke*, who knew that the *Tipperary* had been wrecked so that the mantle of Captain (D) had passed to him. Yet neither he, nor any other destroyer, conveyed this vital news to Jellicoe by wirelessing an enemy report—even when they had a chance to draw breath because the attack drove the head of Scheer's line away to WbyS.* During this lull Allen managed to collect eight of his scattered flotilla and to set a southerly course with the intention of regaining station on Jellicoe's battle fleet. But soon after midnight,

> the hull of a large ship was sighted on the starboard bow not more than half a mile away [remembers one of the *Broke*'s officers]. The Captain immediately gave the order to challenge but almost as he spoke the stranger switched on a vertical string of coloured lights, an unknown signal in our Service. 'Starboard twenty; full speed ahead both; starboard foremost tube fire when your sights come on; all guns green four oh, a battleship'—but the German had evidently been watching our movements and we were too late. [The *Westfalen*] switched on a blaze of searchlights straight in our eyes, then shells could be heard screaming over our heads.

The Sub-Lieutenant of the *Sparrowhawk*, commanded by Lieutenant-Commander S. Hopkins, continues the story of the Fourth Flotilla's second clash with the head of Scheer's line:

> The helm was put over to bring the *Sparrowhawk* round to port, and orders passed to fire the remaining torpedo. The *Broke*, ahead of us, had also put her helm over but, just as we were both turning, [she was] hit by a salvo forward and, to my horror, when she should have eased her helm and steadied to fire a torpedo as we were doing, I saw that she was still swinging very quickly to port [with] her helm jammed. In addition to the enemy's gunfire which was straddling us with every salvo, the *Broke* [was] coming straight for our bridge at 28 knots. I remember shouting a warning to everybody to hold on and to the [forward]

---

* This was the movement mentioned on p. 135. which required the German Commander-in-Chief to order Redlich to turn back towards the Horn Reefs, whereby the *Birmingham* chanced to sight Hipper's battlecruisers temporarily steering the parallel course of S instead of the converging course of SEbyS.

22   *A salvo from the main armament of a German dreadnought*

23   *Scheer's battle fleet at sea*

24   *Jellicoe's flagship,* H.M.S. Iron Duke, *armed with ten 13·5-inch guns*

25   *The German dreadnought* Kronprinz Wilhelm, *armed with ten 12-inch guns*

guns' crew to clear the forecastle, [and], just as she hit us, 'Now'; [but] nothing more till I found myself lying on the forecastle, not of our ship, but of the *Broke* [which] was an absolute shambles.

Before the two vessels separated, the *Sparrowhawk*'s Sub. was able to jump back onboard his own ship. The five following destroyers avoided the cripples but the *Contest*, Lieutenant-Commander E. G. H. Masters, failed to see Hopkins' ship in time and added to her injuries by slicing off several feet of her stern.

The *Broke* was badly damaged and had 42 dead and six missing as well as 34 wounded. Fortunately the forward bulkhead of the foremost boiler-room held so that Allen was able to set course to the northward at slow speed. An hour later, when his hopes of getting away were rising, he sighted two torpedoboats which had become detached from their flotilla. However, 'the Germans appeared even more scared than we were. On approaching to within 500 yards the leader opened fire with her bow gun. We replied with the only remaining one that would bear, and to our astonishment and joy both ships put over their helms and disappeared into the early morning mist.' After this disturbing incident Allen continued his slow passage to the northward until 0600 on 2nd June when, with a long way still to go, he had to face the unpleasant fact that his bulkheads would no longer stand up to punching into a considerable sea from the NW and was obliged to turn his stern to it and steer towards Heligoland. Fortunately the wind and sea moderated towards sunset and he was able to alter course for the Tyne which was safely reached some 24 hours after the *Spitfire*.

The crippled *Sparrowhawk*, being unable to steam, lay where she was, lit by the flames of the burning *Tipperary*. Around 0200 she was seen by a lone German torpedoboat which closed to within 100 yards— but thought better of opening fire and made off to the east. Soon after this the *Tipperary* sank, extinguishing her unwelcome flames, but Hopkins and his crew had another disturbing moment when a new day dawned: a German light cruiser appeared out of the mist about two miles away. The *Sparrowhawk*'s crew prepared to engage with their one remaining gun, but to their astonishment the enemy did not open fire. Moreover, at 0340 'she settled down forward, very slowly, then quietly stood on her head and sank. We had seemed to be absolutely done, no hope whatever, and then this happened; you can imagine what we felt like.' The stranger was, indeed, almost a phantom, the crippled *Elbing* which had been abandoned by Madlung and his crew.

At 0610 there was another alarm, this time for a submarine which turned out to be a carley raft full of men. 'As they managed to paddle nearer we heard them singing, "It's a long, long way to Tipperary", so we knew who they were.' Fifteen of Wintour's crew were rescued. An hour later three British destroyers hove in sight and the *Marksman*, Commander N. A. Sulivan, took the battered *Sparrowhawk* in tow. But both hawsers soon parted and Sullivan was obliged to report that towing was impossible in the prevailing sea. He was ordered to sink the wreck after taking off the surviving members of Hopkins' crew and those fortunate few who had been saved from the *Tipperary*.

Neither Allen nor Hopkins was in a position to report their second encounter with the German First Battle Squadron. But Commander R. B. C. Hutchinson of the *Achates*, who assumed command of the remainder of the Fourth Flotilla, did not do so either, so that the Commander-in-Chief remained in ignorance of the fateful truth, that Scheer's Battle Fleet was heading across his wake. But if this be criticism, there can be nothing but praise for the tenacity with which these six British destroyer captains and their crews opposed the enemy. Nor was their courage without reward; before the *Achates* and two others allowed themselves to be chased away to the NE, they fired their torpedoes, and one struck the *Rostock*, Michelson's flagship, and so disabled her that she had to be taken in tow. Whilst the *Fortune*, Lieutenant-Commander F. G. Terry, belied her name and was sunk, and the *Porpoise*, Commander H. D. Colville, was damaged by a heavy shell but managed to crawl away to safety, the *Ardent*, Lieutenant-Commander G. A. Marsden, sighted

a big ship steaming on the opposite course to us. I attacked at once, and from a very close range our remaining torpedoes were fired, but before I could judge their effect the enemy switched on searchlights. I then became aware that the *Ardent* was taking on a division of German battleships. Our guns were useless against such adversaries; we could do no more than wait for the first salvo. At last it came; shell after shell hit us, our speed diminished and then we stopped. Our three guns ceased firing one by one. I was wounded, but felt no great pain or discomfort though eventually a piece of shell as big as my little finger was taken out of me. [When] the enemy suddenly switched off lights and ceased fire, I could feel the ship sinking and [told] my First Lieutenant to get out the boats and rafts, or what might be left of them, to try and save as many of the crew as possible. A terrible scene of destruction was revealed as I walked aft. Many [had been] killed. I [passed] the word for each man to look out for himself. Then all of a sudden we were again lit by searchlights and the enemy poured in four or five more salvoes at point-blank range. The *Ardent* gave a big lurch, heeled right over and threw me to the ship's side. I flopped over into the sea, grabbing a lifebuoy that was providentially at hand. The *Ardent* slowly sank from view [and], as the smoke and steam cleared, I could see many heads in the water—about 40 or 50. There was no support beyond lifebuoys [etc.] so I was afraid that few of us could survive. I spoke to many and saw most of them die one by one. Not a man showed any fear of death and there was not a murmur, complaint or cry for help. Their joy was, and they talked about it to the end, that they and the *Ardent* had 'done their bit'. After a long, weary while the sun came up. I found a skiff's oar and put it under my arms. I dropped off into a sort of sleep several times, only to be awakened by waves slapping into my face. There was quite a swell. [Finally] I woke to find the *Marksman* close alongside me. I sang out for help and got a welcome and reassuring shout, [then] once again relapsed into unconsciousness [so that] I have no recollection of being got onboard just after 0600.

To his crew, of whom only one survived besides himself, Marsden paid this heartfelt tribute: 'All hands fought the ship with the utmost gallantry till she sank beneath them and then met their death in that composed and happy spirit that I am convinced comes to all those who do their duty to the end.' There were many more in both fleets who earned a like epitaph.

This epic sequence of hard-fought encounters between the Fourth Flotilla and Scheer's Battle Fleet cost Germany two light cruisers against the loss of four British destroyers plus three badly damaged. 'Alone [Wintour's ships] had borne the brunt of the whole German Battle Fleet, and not a man had flinched. Again and again they [had] attacked till nearly every boat had spent all her torpedoes or was a wreck. Such high spirit and skill had they shown that one thing is certain—the failure of the flotilla to achieve [more] was due to no shortcoming in the human factor. It was the power of the weapon [the torpedo fired by surface ships] that had been overrated' (*Corbett*). Scheer's determination to reach the Horn Reefs before dawn was only momentarily checked and, although the darkness had been rent time and again during the best part of an hour by the flashes of heavy gunfire, not so much as a whisper of what was happening reached Jellicoe. One may understand why none of the British destroyer captains who were so hotly engaged by German dreadnoughts made an enemy report. But between 2315 and 0015 there were others who could have told their Commander-in-Chief that the High Seas Fleet was crossing his wake. From about 2200 the torpedoed *Marlborough* had been unable to maintain 17 knots, with the result that her division had slowly dropped astern of station. Since Burney did not inform Evan-Thomas of his flagship's difficulty, the Fifth Battle Squadron, which was keeping station on the *Marlborough*, also dropped astern. Scheer's converging course thus crossed only three miles astern of these seven battleships which consequently saw more of the Fourth Flotilla's action than the rest of the British battle fleet. This is especially true of the *Malaya* at the rear of Evan-Thomas's squadron. According to Boyle's report: '2340. Three points abaft the starboard beam observed what appeared to be an attack by our destroyers on some enemy ships steering the same way as ours. The leading ship had two masts, two funnels and a conspicuous crane—apparently "Westfalen class." She *was* the *Westfalen*, leading Scheer's line. All the *Malaya*'s guns were trained on her and the Gunnery Officer asked permission to open fire, but Boyle refused; like Arbuthnot on 16th December 1914, he argued that what he could see must be visible in the *Barham* two ships ahead; the *Malaya* must await orders from Evan-Thomas. On the same false assumption Boyle made no enemy report; but the *Barham* and *Valiant*, and Burney's ships, only saw what appeared to be 'constant attacks by torpedo craft on ships [which they could not identify] first to the westward and then to the northward'.

Stationed next to port of the Fourth Flotilla was the Thirteenth, so that at about 2330 Farie saw heavy firing on the *Champion*'s starboard beam. He immediately increased to high speed, and 'hauled out to the eastwards [because] I was unable to attack the enemy with any of [my] own flotilla [whilst] our own forces [were] between me and the enemy'. By doing this without signal, when leading a flotilla which was showing no lights, Farie lost touch with all except the *Moresby* and *Obdurate*. Moreover, he obliged the British flotillas to the east of him to move further in that direction, thus opening a road for the German fleet, whilst his own two rear ships, the *Menace* and *Nonsuch*, were nearly rammed and sunk by the *Frankfurt* and *Pillau*. Nonetheless, since the Grand Fleet flotillas had not been organized and trained to carry out co-ordinated night attacks, Farie's action is understandable; his failure to report what he had seen and heard is another matter. There were, however, worse examples of missed opportunities by

British ships. Soon after the German battlecruisers had moved to the rear of Scheer's Battle Fleet, the damaged *Seydlitz* reported that she could not maintain 16 knots. Ordered to make his own way to the Horn Reefs, Egidy steered out in an easterly direction. Soon afterwards Hipper's flagship, the *Moltke*, lost touch and also steered more to the east. As a result both battlecruisers had individual encounters with the Grand Fleet. At 2230 Karpf sighted Jerram's Second Battle Squadron, and was seen by the *Thunderer* at the rear. But Captain Fergusson neither reported the *Moltke* nor opened fire 'as it was considered inadvisable to show up [our] battle fleet'; Karpf was allowed to veer away to the west. Too soon he resumed his original course so that Jerram's ships were again sighted ahead at 2255. This time none saw Hipper's flagship so that she again eluded them. Once more Karpf turned towards the Horn Reefs and at 2320 was frustrated for the third time. Hipper then told Karpf to steer to the south whereby the *Moltke* passed clear ahead of the Grand Fleet at about 0130 and so reached safety. The *Moltke*'s radio being out of action, no reports of these encounters reached Scheer until Hipper fell in with torpedoboat *G39* at 0227. They were then too late to be of use; but even if they had been transmitted at the time, they would only have told Scheer that by steering SEbyS he was passing astern of the British Battle Fleet.

The *Seydlitz* had a more astonishing escape. Around midnight she was sighted by the *Marlborough* who identified her as 'a large ship' but did nothing; by the *Revenge* next astern where Captain Kiddle challenged her and was satisfied by the wrong reply; and by the *Agincourt* at the rear where Captain Doughty 'did not challenge her so as not to give our division's position away'. The light cruisers *Boadicea* and *Fearless* also saw the *Seydlitz* but followed the example of Burney's captains, 'it being too late to fire a torpedo when she could be identified' (*Roper*). Egidy, with thousands of tons of water in his ship's battered hull was thus allowed to wander safely past four British battleships, not to mention a flotilla of destroyers, to reach the Horn Reefs in the morning.

By 0030 the head of Schmidt's squadron was to the east of Jellicoe's Battle Fleet, but there were still three groups of British destroyers between Scheer and safety. The more westerly of these should have comprised the seven boats of Goldsmith's merged Ninth and Tenth Flotillas, led by the *Lydiard*, which would have passed clear ahead of the converging German line. However, unknown to Goldsmith, the six boats of the Thirteenth Flotilla, which had lost touch with the

Champion, had joined him, and the four rear ships of this extended line sighted the German First Battle Squadron as they passed close ahead. The first two identified their opponents too late to attack. The *Petard*, coming next, was in an admirable position to do so, but

> had fired all her torpedoes in the day attack [recalls her captain, Lieutenant-Commander E. C. O. Thomson]. There was nothing we could do but get away. We increased to full speed and altered to port to clear the enemy's stem. As soon as we had passed ahead of [the *Westfalen*] she switched her searchlights on us; we saw the flashes of [her] secondary armament, felt the ship tremble slightly and guessed we had been hit aft. The second ship in the line—we could now see four—joined in [and a] salvo struck us forward, but luckily missed the bridge. German searchlights were [then] switched off us and trained on the *Turbulent*, my next astern [and] she was rammed and sunk by [the *Westfalen*].* We escaped without further incident [having been] hit six times, [one having] killed or severely wounded the crew of the after 4-inch gun, wrecked all the officers' cabins and killed the Surgeon Probationer at the moment when his services were most required.

For most of the eleven British destroyers which escaped unscathed from this encounter, 'it all happened so suddenly that we hardly realized what was taking place. It somehow did not strike us [in the *Nicator*] that this was the German fleet breaking through the line at the weakest point'. It is not so easy to understand the failure of the *Petard* and her sisters, which did identify their opponents, to wireless a report to Jellicoe, most of whose battleships had no more to say of the night than Captain Bruen of the *Bellerophon*, stationed three ships from the rear of Sturdee's Fourth Battle Squadron: 'During the first watch there was quite a lot of firing going on to the NE and a cruiser seemed to be on fire pretty badly. At about 2340 there was further firing astern and for the first hour or so of the middle watch there was intermittent firing on the port quarter. *Otherwise the night passed without incident*.'† In the *Lion*, some five miles further ahead Chatfield 'expected any moment to be attacked by [torpedoboats], but no exciting incident occurred with the exception of *many indications that other portions of the fleet were not having such a peaceful time as we were*'.† But in the *Iron Duke*, according to Dreyer, no one supposed it to be more than 'German cruisers and destroyers trying to break through our destroyer screen to attack our battle fleet'.

* Lieutenant-Commander D. Stuart and his whole crew were lost in this collision.
† Author's italics.

A greater tragedy was enacted in the Admiralty. At 2315 Room 40 deciphered two signals; the first, from Scheer timed 2232, read: 'Main fleet steering SEbyS'. Perhaps this was not significantly different from the course which the War Room had transmitted to Jellicoe half an hour before, but when read in conjunction with the other which Michelson had made to all his torpedoboats at the same time—'Be assembled by 0200 at Horn Reefs or course round Skaw'—the War Room held vital intelligence (despite Room 40's accidental omission of the words 'with our main body' after 'assembled') which could have reached Jellicoe by midnight and enabled him to forestall Scheer's arrival at the Horn Reefs light. Fate decreed otherwise; in the continued absence of the First Sea Lord and the Chief of the War Staff, Thomas Jackson did nothing with it. Nor were the following further messages from Scheer, which were deciphered later, relayed to Jellicoe: the first made at 2306 (deciphered 2350) gave the position and course of his main body; the second made at 2330 (deciphered by midnight) and the third at 2336 (deciphered at 0005) signalled small adjustments to the course of the German Battle Fleet. Two more giving Scheer's position at 0043 and at 0103 (deciphered at 0120 and 0125), which might have reached Jellicoe in time to influence events, were likewise not passed to the *Iron Duke*. One must wonder why the Director of Operations troubled to tell Jellicoe at 0148 that U-boats were coming out of German ports and to give him the position of the sinking *Lützow*, and at 0312 the position in which the *Elbing* had been abandoned since, by comparison, these pieces of intelligence were of very limited value.

Goldsmith's ships had so nearly passed clear ahead of the German battle fleet that the Twelfth Flotilla, led by Captain Stirling in the *Faulknor*, must have done so but for the chance that it was keeping station on Burney's lagging division and so was more than ten miles astern of the *Iron Duke*:

At 0143 [noted one of the *Obedient*'s officers], as daylight was appearing, a line of ships was sighted on our starboard beam, steering about ESE. Owing to the mist we could not determine whether they were enemy or not, but our doubts were soon dispelled by one of them challenging us [incorrectly]. We were [leading] the division nearest the enemy [so] our Captain [Commander G. W. Campbell] decided to attack. We altered to starboard to do so but just afterwards observed that the enemy had turned away about six points [so] turned back to rejoin the *Faulknor* [which] had increased to 23 knots, and altered 16 points to starboard. The enemy was now clearly visible on our port side, dreadnoughts leading and pre-dreadnoughts following. Conditions were nearly ideal for an attack, as it was too light for searchlights to be of much use and yet, with the mist as an added cloak, sufficiently dark to make the laying of guns on fast moving targets difficult. At 0205 we fired our first torpedo, being then abreast the fourth ship of their line, at a range of 2,000 to 3,000 yards. At the same moment fire was opened upon us from all calibres of guns. Just as it seemed that we must be hit, and when we thought our torpedo must have missed, there came our reward. Right amidships in the *Pommern* appeared a dull red ball of fire. It spread fore and aft [and] flared up the masts in big red tongues of flame, uniting in a black cloud of smoke and sparks. Then one saw the ends of the ship come up as though her back was broken before the mist shut her out from view. In the silence that followed a voice on our bridge was heard to say: 'Pity the poor devils, they ain't drawn their money's worth'. A heavy fire continued to be directed at us and the *Nessus* and *Onslaught* were hit.* We increased speed and commenced to zigzag which saved us. Further torpedoes were fired at the enemy [by the *Maenad*'s division] but nothing could be seen of the result, and the mist quickly shut out the ships from view.

Stirling's attack was the most skilfully conducted in the whole battle, at least on the British side, even though only six of his destroyers managed to fire a total of 17 torpedoes whilst the others were driven off by accurate German gunfire. It cost Scheer one of his pre-dreadnoughts with Captain Bölken and all his company. Moreover, in sharp contrast to previous incidents, Stirling made as many as three enemy reports. Unfortunately, for no certain reason—perhaps a damaged aerial in the *Faulknor*, perhaps enemy jamming—neither of the first two was received by the *Iron Duke* or any other ship, and the third only by the *Marksman*, one of Stirling's own flotilla. Had it been otherwise, had Jellicoe received these signals and turned his Battle Fleet at once, he could have reached a position near the German minefields from which to open fire on Scheer's Battle Fleet at 10,000 yards at 0330. Even if he had turned a little later he would have picked off some of the damaged German ships which were unable to keep up with their main body. As it was, the long-drawn-out battle was almost over; Jellicoe's expedient of using his flotillas to prevent the High Seas Fleet crossing his stern during the night had failed; worse than this, it had left him in astonishing ignorance of the very fact that Scheer had so successfully eluded his grasp.

* The latter's captain, Lieutenant-Commander A. G. Onslow, being killed.

Scheer's unshakeable resolve had taken the High Seas Fleet across the path of the Grand Fleet at no greater cost than the loss of one pre-dreadnought and three light cruisers. Nonetheless, at daybreak, when his battle fleet saw nothing of the enemy,

> reports showed that the First Scouting Group could not sustain a serious fight. The leading ships of the Third Battle Squadron could not have fought for any length of time owing to shortage of ammunition. The *Frankfurt*, *Pillau* and *Regensburg* were the only fast light cruisers now available. In such misty weather there was no depending on aerial reconnaissance. There was, therefore, no certain prospect of defeating the enemy; an encounter and the consequences had to be left to chance. I therefore abandoned the idea of further operations and ordered a return to port.

But at 0230 the minefields behind which the High Seas Fleet would be safe were still an hour's steaming away.

On board the *Neptune* one of her midshipmen noted the confidence with which the Grand Fleet was imbued as the sun rose. 'At 0200 we were all back at our action stations. The visibility gave promise of a better day. We had plenty of ammunition left and felt that, given the chance, we could make short work of what remained of the enemy. The guns had been left loaded and were ready to start again.' Jellicoe still supposed the enemy Battle Fleet to be to the westward; nor was he dismayed when dawn revealed no German vessel in sight since the morning mist limited visibility to four miles. He was, however, concerned to discover the extent to which his squadrons and flotillas had been scattered. Seven of his battleships had dropped well astern during the night; except for Le Mesurier's Fourth Light Cruiser Squadron, the battlecruisers and cruisers which he needed to search for the enemy, were out of sight ahead; and he had no destroyers with which to counter enemy torpedoboat attacks or, potentially more menacing, to deal with the U-boats of which the Admiralty had warned him. 'All this,' he wrote, 'rendered it undesirable to close the Horn Reefs at daylight as had been my intention. It was obviously necessary to collect the battle fleet and the destroyers before renewing the action.' Believing Scheer to be to the north of west rather than to the south, he reversed course at 0230 and, maintaining his cruising speed of 17 knots, deployed his battle fleet into single line ahead, after wirelessing his position and intentions to Beatty and other senior officers and ordering them to conform.

The High Seas Fleet would, therefore, have avoided further action but for Farie's 2330 decision to turn away to the east instead of following up Wintour's spirited attack, when the *Champion* had lost touch with her Thirteenth Flotilla except for the *Moresby* and *Obdurate*. Because daylight made it possible to distinguish friend from foe, Farie turned towards the sound of gunfire from Stirling's dawn engagement. With his force augmented by the *Marksman* and *Maenad* from the the Twelfth Flotilla, he sighted the rear four 'Deutschlands' of Scheer's line to the west at 0230. He did not, however, seize the chance to make an attack; he turned the *Champion* away to the east. But Lieutenant-Commander R. V. Alison of the *Moresby* refused to follow his leader: displaying the same initiative as had animated so many British destroyer captains, in sharp contrast to their seniors in Jellicoe's battleships, he 'considered action imperative, hoisted "compass west" [and] hauled out to port, firing a torpedo at 0237. A concussion shook the ship two minutes later. I feel certain that the torpedo hit something.' It did, though such a gallant attempt deserved to achieve more than sending the torpedoboat *V4* to the bottom.

This was the last that any British ship saw of a major German unit before the head of Scheer's line reached the Horn Reefs light at 0330 and turned south down the swept channel. But not all the High Seas Fleet reached the Jade without further incident. At about 0330 the *Champion* and her four destroyers sighted the four enemy torpedoboats which were carrying the 1250 members of the crew of the sunken *Lützow*. Closing to 3,000 yards both sides opened fire and the *G40* was quickly disabled. As quickly Farie lost his opponents in the mist so that they were able to take their crippled sister in tow. Reinforced by the *Regensburg*, this small German force was again sighted forty minutes later, this time by the damaged *Dublin* which, since losing touch with her squadron, had had the alarming experience of passing alone through the High Seas Fleet during the night, fortunately without being detected. However, before either Scott or Heinrich could decide to open fire they were lost to each other in the mist, so that the *G40* eventually reached harbour. The crippled *Rostock*, which was also being towed towards the Horn Reefs, was less fortunate; her escorts were sufficiently alarmed by a zeppelin report of the proximity of British battleships to decide to scuttle their charge after taking off Michelson and his flagship's crew. At 0520, Schmidt's flagship, the pre-dreadnought *Ostfriesland*, struck a mine laid by the *Abdiel*—not in the field which she had laid that night, but in an earlier one sown on 5th May. Captain Natzmer's ship was not, however, seriously damaged; nor did this incident deter Scheer from holding on for the Jade where, with a sense of relief shared by all but a few of his officers and men, he arrived early in the forenoon*; though Behncke's flagship, the *König*, was drawing so much water forward that she was delayed until a rising tide allowed her to clear the Amrun Bank. The battlecruiser *Seydlitz* had a more difficult passage; drawing 42 feet forward, she grounded off the Horn Reefs. Fortunately Egidy was able to clear this obstacle before any British ship came within range. His ship subsequently stuck fast on the Amrun Bank until salvage steamers came to her aid—and they had a 32-hour struggle before they managed to tow the *Seydlitz* into harbour stern first.

A zeppelin report has been mentioned. Five of these craft had left their sheds at 1130 on the 31st for a reconnaissance of an arc with a radius of 200 miles from the Horn Reefs; but, despite much prompting by wireless after the *Elbing*'s report of sighting the *Galatea*, none succeeded in getting within 30 miles of either the British or German fleets before being recalled at 1800. Ironically enough, Scheer's request for a dawn reconnaissance on the 1st was not received by his airship commander. Nonetheless Captain Strasser sent six zeppelins out at midnight. Four achieved no more than their sisters on the previous day. *L24* confused the issue by reporting the German torpedoboats which were returning home by way of the Skagerrak as British, and by an even more erroneous report of phantom British battleships in Jammer Bay which is on Denmark's north-west coast. Only *L11* achieved anything; at 0319, recalls one of the *Neptune*'s officers, 'a zeppelin suddenly appeared out of the morning haze and steered towards us. An order was passed to "X" turret to fire one round at its maximum elevation. Our next ahead fired a whole salvo and other ships started in. The airship lifted its nose disdainfully to the morning breeze and disappeared, and a signal was received ordering us not to waste ammunition.' *L11* continued to shadow the Grand Fleet for more than an hour, at 0340 approaching the *Indomitable* so close that she received a

---

* The High Seas Fleet passed safely over three British submarines lying off the Vyl lightship because they had been sent there as part of Jellicoe's original plan for drawing the enemy out, with orders to remain on the bottom until 2nd June, so that they knew nothing of Jutland until they returned to Yarmouth on 9th June.

salvo from her 12-inch guns, but her reports only confirmed Scheer's wisdom in gaining the safety of the Horn Reefs and his decision to return to harbour without seeking to renew the battle. The U-boats which had left Borkum Roads at 2045 on the 31st achieved even less: only one out of six sighted anything. *U46* made an unsuccessful attack on the *Marlborough* as she was being escorted back to the Tyne after Burney had transferred his flag to the *Revenge* at 0230.

Since Beatty had not received such intelligence as the Admiralty had wirelessed to Jellicoe during the night and had been too far ahead to see much of the destroyer actions, he did not share his Commander-in-Chief's appreciation of Scheer's whereabouts. He believed the enemy would have made such speed towards one of his southern routes to the Jade, that he would be to the south of west rather than to the north. The Battlecruiser Fleet held on in the high hopes of making a sighting until shortly after 0300 before conforming with the Battle Fleet's turn to N. Even then, Beatty was so inclined towards his own view that he signalled Jellicoe at 0404: 'Submit I may sweep SW to locate enemy'. Only ten minutes earlier, however, Jellicoe had received news that dashed all his hopes: from a signal originated in the Admiralty at 0330, based on messages deciphered by Room 40, the British Commander-in-Chief learned that the German Battle Fleet had been only 16 miles from the Horn Reefs at 0230—30 miles to the NE of the *Iron Duke*— steering SEbyS at 16 knots. Since an hour-and-a-half had elapsed, he could reach only one conclusion and he signalled the bitter pill to Beatty: 'Enemy fleet has returned to harbour'. Thus to both Admirals' officers and men came the gradual realization, the maturing disappointment, that 'we should not see the High Seas Fleet that day: there was to be no completion of yesterday's work'.

At 0415 the British Commander-in-Chief re-formed his battle fleet into its day cruising order. Both he and Beatty, who was in visual touch by 0520, still hoped that they might locate the *Lützow* or the *Elbing*. But, as their ships swept the battleground, 'the only signs of the enemy were hundreds of their drowned bluejackets in their life-saving waist-coats, floating near the great smears of oil and wreckage that marked the grave of some ship' (*a 'New Zealand' officer*). There were as many tell-tale relics of the British vessels which had been sunk—but nothing more. By 1100 Jellicoe was left with only one possible decision: he informed the Admiralty that the Grand Fleet was returning to harbour. And as the British ships steamed towards Scapa and Rosyth, where they were to come to anchor early next morning, many enacted the last poignant scene. Onboard the *Lion*

> the removal of the poor charred bodies from 'Q' turret was a very sad sight. For the burial, the Admiral, Flag Captain, and all available officers and men were on the quarterdeck, the Captain reading the committal prayer. There were two parties of bearers, and a plank, port and starboard right aft on which the bodies were placed in turn under the Union Flag, one each side being slid off on to the sea at the same time. There were 95 poor mutilated forms in their hammocks, shotted at the feet, including those of six officers. The band played one or two hymns and the Dead March during the half-hour the sad ceremony lasted. We could see other ships similarly engaged. (*Engineer Commander Rundle*)

'I mourn the loss of brave men, many of them personal friends of my own, who have fallen in their country's cause,' King George V signalled to Jellicoe on 3rd June. 'Yet even more do I regret that the German High Seas Fleet was enabled by the misty weather to evade the full consequences of an encounter they have always professed to desire, but for which, when the opportunity arrived, they showed no inclination.'

6

Who Won?

'*Not in the thick of the fight,*
  Not in the press of the odds,
 Do the heroes come to their height . . .
  That stands over till peace.'
                    Kipling on Jutland in 1916

'[When Jellicoe] assumed the name of "Viscount Scapa"*
there was a good deal of scoffing that an admiral should take
the name of a desolate place where his fleet had remained at
anchor almost continuously for four years. Yet by those
four years the British Fleet exerted the decisive pressure
which ended in our whole fighting fleet being led to Scapa
Flow where it now lies on the sea bottom.'
                    Commander von Hase

THE BRITISH casualties at Jutland were much heavier than the
German: out of some 60,000 officers and men who manned the 151
ships of the Grand Fleet, 6,097 were killed; in contrast the High Seas
Fleet, of 99 ships manned by some 36,000 officers and men, lost only
2,551. (The numbers wounded on both sides were almost the same:
British, 510; German, 507.) But the victor of a naval action is not
judged by lives lost.

The ships sunk are best tabulated:

	British	*German*
Battleship (pre-dreadnought)	—	1
Battlecruisers	3	1
Armoured cruisers	3	—
Light cruisers	—	4
Destroyers/Torpedoboats	8	5
Total	14	11

* He was created Viscount Jellicoe of Scapa in January 1918. In contrast Beatty
received an earldom in 1919, with the additional title of Baron of the North Sea.
Similar justice was not done to Jellicoe until 1925.

Germany claimed a victory from these figures, especially the number of British heavy ships lost (to which Scheer mistakenly added the *Warspite*). But on 2nd June the Grand Fleet was still twice as strong as the High Seas Fleet, with 31 dreadnoughts against 18 and seven battlecruisers to match four. More important, within 12 hours of returning to Scapa and Rosyth, Jellicoe could report that he had 26 battleships and six battlecruisers at four hours' notice for sea; only the *Marlborough* and *Warspite* had to be taken in hand for immediate repairs; the *Barham*, *Malaya*, *Lion* and *Tiger* could wait until the four ships already refitting (see p. 64 n.1 and n.2) returned from dockyard hands. Scheer could make no such favourable report: the *König*, *Grosser Kurfürst* and *Markgraf* had to be repaired without waiting for the *König Albert* and *Bayern* (see p. 64 n.3), whilst all four battlecruisers were so badly damaged that the last was not ready for service until December (whereas the last British ship, the *Marlborough*, completed repairs at the beginning of August). With its cruiser strength cut to six, against Jellicoe's 30, the High Seas Fleet was not fit for sea and action for nearly two months.

The British losses were so much heavier because the *Queen Mary*, *Indefatigable* and *Invincible* were each destroyed by a single salvo, whereas the crippled *Lützow* almost survived the battle before being sunk by her escort. The explanation was quickly revealed by the *Lion*'s 'Q' turret (see p. 78). The pity of it is that the Admiralty did not appreciate the importance of protecting magazines against cordite flash from the near-destruction of the armoured cruiser *Kent* at the Falkland Islands,* so that the necessary improvements to the British ships could have been put in hand before Jutland: nine turrets in Hipper's battlecruisers were pierced by British shells on 31st May, some being burnt out by the resulting fires, but there was no magazine explosion. This, however, was not the only reason why the *Seydlitz* and *Derfflinger*, *König* and *Grosser Kurfürst*, to name the four worst damaged, survived the battering to which they were subjected. The Germans had subdivided their ships into a larger number of watertight compartments; their latest dreadnoughts had six engine-rooms and six boiler-rooms compared with three of each in the British. Nor were they content with this measure of protection against extensive flooding from hits on or below the waterline; the *Seydlitz*'s damage control organization stands out in contrast to that of the *Iron Duke* where the

---

* To be fair, the lesson was not so obvious from the *Kent*'s experience as it was from the *Seydlitz*'s at the Dogger Bank.

26   *Nearly lost at Jutland: the German battlecruiser* Seydlitz *on fire*

27   *The badly damaged* Seydlitz *in dock at Wilhelmshaven after the action*

28 *Beatty's flagship, the battlecruiser* Lion, *on the day after Jutland, showing her damaged 'Q' turret (amidships)*

29 *After Jutland: the damaged British light cruiser* Chester

Executive Officer, who should have been in charge of it, was stationed in the foretop as principal spotting officer. Scheer's heavy ships had a further advantage; Fisher's refusal to allocate naval funds for new docks required British constructors to restrict the beam of their dreadnoughts to the width of those already available; Tirpitz built the docks needed to give his dreadnoughts greater stability. Moreover, since the Germans accepted a smaller calibre of gun for most of their battleships and battle-cruisers, they were able to allow them more armour. The following typical figures show how much nearer German dreadnoughts approached Tirpitz's requirement that they should be unsinkable gun platforms than contemporary British vessels:

	Iron Duke	König	Lion	Derfflinger
Displacement (tons)	25,000	25,390	26,350	26,180
Length (feet)	580	573	660	689
Beam (feet)	90	97	88	95
Main armament	10–13·5″	10–12″	8–13·5″	8–12″
Armour (sides) (max.)	12″	14″	9″	12″
(turrets) (max.)	11″	14″	9″	11″
Max. speed (knots)	21	21	27	26·5

The advantage conferred on the German ships by their thicker armour was not, however, as great as it should have been; post-war trials on the *Baden* showed that her armour was not up to British standards.

So long as battles were fought at near point-blank range, ships were best protected by armouring their sides. Although deck armour against plunging projectiles acquired a comparable importance when ranges increased, this was so little appreciated by both British and German constructors that neither's ships' decks exceeded 2½ inches. But this was more to the Grand Fleet's disadvantage than its opponent's because of the deficiencies in British gunnery. One was the poor shooting by Beatty's battlecruisers which bore the brunt of the action as the following table shows* (see also p. 84n. and p. 93n.):

	Rounds fired (12-inch and above)	Hits obtained	Rounds fired to obtain one hit
British battlecruisers	1650	26	64
British battleships	2626	98	26

This difference was largely responsible for the gunnery efficiency of the High Seas Fleet appearing to be higher than that of the Grand Fleet:

* In this and the subsequent tables the rounds fired and hits obtained are as near as can be calculated since they can only be estimated in the case of ships sunk

	Guns, 11-inch and above	Hits obtained	Hits per gun
British ships	344	124	·36
German ships	244	120	·53

In fact there was little difference between the standards achieved by the *battleships* of the two fleets:

	Guns, 11-inch and above	Hits obtained	Hits per gun
British battleships	296	110	·37
German battleships	200	80	·4

Hipper's comment on the other British deficiency has been quoted (p. 84); at the Admiralty before the war Jellicoe realized the need for armour-piercing shells which would be effective when they struck at the oblique angle of the trajectory of long-range fire, but he had not been Director of Naval Ordnance for long enough to ensure that they were provided*; more British shells broke up on impact, instead of piercing and detonating, than German ones. These faults in the British Fleet do not, however, assist in determining the victor from the number of ships lost and seriously damaged; by comparison with the Nile from which only two of the French fleet escaped, with Trafalgar where Villeneuve lost two-thirds of his ships-of-the-line, or with Tsushima where Rozhdestvensky's Baltic Fleet was annihilated, Jutland was indecisive. But 'victory is measured not by a comparison of casualties and losses, not by tactical incidents in the battle, *but only by results*' †(*Hankey*).

Scheer's purpose was limited to weakening a stronger enemy by engaging no more than a part of his fleet; Jellicoe's was to do as much damage as he could to the High Seas Fleet without subjecting his own to undue risk, especially from underwater attack. The first round went to Scheer because Hipper's force, having made a chance contact with Beatty's, enticed it within range of the German Battle Fleet. The second was Jellicoe's because Beatty lured an unsuspecting Scheer north until he was surprised by the whole British Battle Fleet. The fact that the British Battlecruiser Fleet achieved this, its chief purpose when operating with Jellicoe's Battle Fleet, is a sufficient answer to those who assert that Beatty was decisively defeated during the first

---

* Responsibility for the design of naval shell was vested in the Ordnance Committee, an inter-Service body with a plethora of commitments.

† Author's italics.

phase of the battle. Points were equal in the third round; although Jellicoe was successful in engaging the High Seas Fleet on a course which cut it off from its base, he failed to follow Scheer when he first recoiled from this onslaught, and again when his opponent offered him another chance by an ill-judged return to the east. The fourth round was Scheer's because during the night he escaped from the trap into which he had fallen and reached safety by dawn. So much, two rounds to one, stands to the Imperial German Navy's credit. Though such a recent creation, its ships and equipment proved superior to the British in several important respects, whilst its crews were as well—in some ways better—trained. Many of its captains likewise showed themselves to be as competent—some more so; nor was their conduct marred by the inhumanity which characterized the U-boat campaign. More important, in Scheer they had a Commander-in-Chief who was a determined fighter and Jellicoe's equal as a tactician, his one major mistake being compensated by the manner of his escape; whilst in Hipper they had the ablest admiral on either side in the whole war.

But what of Jellicoe's purpose, for which his officers and men fought with so much courage, not least those in the engine- and boiler-rooms who are so often forgotten, all of whom were so bitterly disappointed by the result? 'We had them stone cold and we let them go. To wait all that time and then turn away from them instead of towards them was sickening. They gave us our chance and we weren't allowed to take it' (*a Grand Fleet captain, quoted by Richmond*). After waiting for nearly two years Jellicoe was at last able to make contact with the High Seas Fleet. With masterly skill he deployed 27 dreadnoughts against 16. The poor visibility, and the few hours remaining before dark, favoured an enemy unwilling to stand and fight; nonetheless he damaged his opponent to an extent which dismayed Scheer at a cost which the Grand Fleet could well afford. Above all Jutland was not limited to four rounds; there was a fifth after dawn on 1st June, albeit a bloodless one: 'On the morning that followed the battle Jellicoe found himself in undisputed possession of the North Sea without a sign of an enemy and to all intents and purposes this state of affairs continued' (*Hankey*). 'Germany narrowly escaped a crushing defeat. It was clear to every thinking person that this battle must, and would, be the last one' (*Berliner Tageblatt*). Neutral opinion was expressed by a New York newspaper: 'The German Fleet has assaulted its jailor, but it is still in jail'.

Thus the Grand Fleet's blockade remained unbroken. But, contrary to what is often said, the High Seas Fleet did not remain in harbour for the rest of the war. Scheer soon realized that his officers and men were not so easily convinced that they had gained a victory as were the German people; their flight from the fleet they had been trained to fight, and the damage their ships had sustained affected their morale. To restore it, he planned another sortie two-and-a-half months after Jutland, when he sailed two battlecruisers, supported by 18 dreadnoughts, for a dawn bombardment of Sunderland. Forewarned by Room 40, the Admiralty ordered the Grand Fleet of 27 dreadnoughts and six battlecruisers to sea on 18th August. At 1345 next day Jellicoe, after being delayed for two hours by U-boats, was sufficiently confident of making contact to ready his fleet for action. But the devilry of chance denied him battle; Scheer was already steaming away from him. Unlike 31st May, the Admiralty had ordered the Harwich Force out and, when a scouting zeppelin reported this as including a squadron of battleships, Scheer turned SE in pursuit of these phantoms. By the time he realized his mistake, it was too late for him to carry out his intended bombardment so he turned for home. Tyrwhitt made contact at 1745 but had insufficient force to do more than shadow the enemy, when Jellicoe was too far away to be able to come to his support.

Both sides suffered losses from submarine attack in this abortive operation: the light cruisers *Nottingham* and *Falmouth* were sunk and the dreadnought *Westfalen* damaged. Consequently the Admiralty again endorsed Jellicoe's strategy: the Grand Fleet, in which it would take a year to remedy the material deficiencies revealed by Jutland, was vital to the Allied cause; the High Seas Fleet was of only secondary importance to Germany and could be subjected to greater risks. Only in exceptional circumstances—a threat of invasion, or an attack on the Thames or the Straits of Dover—was the British Battle Fleet to come south of the Horn Reefs. When Room 40 warned that Scheer intended another sortie on 18th October, the Grand Fleet was not immediately ordered to face possible U-boat attack; it was only brought to short notice for steam. Nor was it required to sail; when a British submarine patrolling the Heligoland Bight fired a torpedo into the light cruiser *München* a few hours after the High Seas Fleet left the Jade, Scheer feared a trap and returned to harbour.

From the disappointing results of these two post-Jutland sorties, Scheer appreciated that his chances of trapping only a part of the Grand

Fleet were too small to justify further raids against British ports. Still obsessed with the 'fleet in being' concept, the Kaiser agreed. In the same month, December 1916, Lloyd George's Cabinet decided that the seriousness of the U-boat threat required the appointment of Jellicoe as First Sea Lord. He was thus at the Admiralty when the Kaiser, pressed by Hindenburg and Ludendorff, accepted Scheer's contention that the Grand Fleet's unyielding blockade must be countered by the only maritime weapon against which it was no defence; 'that even the most favourable issue of a battle on the high seas will not compel England to make peace. A victorious termination of the war can only be attained by destroying the economic existence of Great Britain by the employment of submarines against commerce.' On 1st February 1917, unrestricted submarine warfare was again declared, 'when the High Seas Fleet was reduced to the hilt of the weapon whose sharp blade was the U-boat' (*Scheer*); when, that is, the British were unable to close the Heligoland Bight completely against the passage of U-boats by minefields, because a German 'fleet in being' prevented these from being patrolled by destroyers. This indirect result of Jutland, with all its implications for neutral countries, was nearly successful; shipping losses rose so steeply that British food reserves were reduced to a six weeks' supply; so, too, was oil fuel so that the movements of the Grand Fleet had to be restricted. But it was not decisive; when the United States joined the Allies on 6th April, the British Navy was reinforced by so many destroyers that Jellicoe, and the fresh blood from the Grand Fleet with which he had invigorated the Naval Staff, initiated a major change; instead of the largely futile method of protecting merchant ships by patrolling the trade routes, they began to sail in escorted convoys. This quickly cut the number of ships lost.

Beatty succeeded Jellicoe in command of the Grand Fleet but, notwithstanding his aggressive leadership of the battlecruisers, he did not suggest any major change in the Grand Fleet's role. His ability to maintain the blockade of Germany was not to be hazarded by attrition by U-boat attack, even though the loss of the *Vanguard** was more than compensated by a squadron of six dreadnoughts flying the Stars and Stripes of the U.S.A. But he made one significant innovation: in April 1917 he began running the Scandinavian trade, for whose safety he was responsible, in convoy. In addition to an anti-submarine

* Destroyed at Scapa in 1917 by the explosion of unstable cordite.

escort of two destroyers and a number of trawlers, he gave each a covering force of light cruisers as protection against German surface craft. It was six months before Scheer seized this chance to assist the U-boat campaign without risking the High Seas Fleet; on 17th October the light cruisers *Brummer* and *Bremse* descended upon a convoy bound for Lerwick from Bergen, and sank ten out of 12 merchant ships after overwhelming the destroyers *Mary Rose* and *Strongbow*. Two months later he repeated this foray with four large destroyers, all six merchant ships in the convoy being sunk together with the destroyer *Partridge*. On both occasions the Germans eluded the covering British cruisers.

These enemy successes were offset by another engagement further south in the North Sea. The numerous minefields laid in the Heligoland Bight, as one of many British anti-submarine measures, brought Scheer's minesweepers as much as 150 miles to seaward. When their destroyer escorts were attacked by Tyrwhitt's force, the German Commander-in-Chief added battleships. To catch these Beatty sent Napier with the big cruisers *Courageous* and *Glorious* and two light cruiser squadrons, supported by the Battlecruiser Force* and the First Battle Squadron, down to the Horn Reefs. At dawn on 17th November, in low visibility, they discovered four German light cruisers and pursued them until 0930, when Napier judged the mine risk too great and recalled his larger ships. But Rear-Admiral Phillimore in the battlecruiser *Repulse* had not forgotten Nelson's example: turning a blind eye to the signal, his flagship continued to support the light cruisers until they sighted the expected German dreadnoughts. Under their fire the British ships turned back, hoping to lure their more powerful opponents out to where the First Battle Squadron was waiting. Unfortunately, Scheer's ships were not to be tempted so far, and the British force was obliged to withdraw without much damage to either side.

Had this offensive operation been repeated it might have achieved a notable success; carrier-borne aircraft attacks on the Tondern zeppelin sheds certainly did, compared with the pre-Jutland ones. But in January 1918 Beatty suggested, and the War Cabinet agreed, that after the complete failure of the previous autumn's Allied offensive in Flanders, the situation was too serious to justify provoking a fleet

---

* On becoming Commander-in-Chief, Beatty changed the title of the Battlecruiser Fleet, in which Pakenham had succeeded him, to make clear that it was not an independent command.

action, notwithstanding the Grand Fleet's superiority of 43 dreadnoughts and battlecruisers to Scheer's 24. Subject to maintaining the
blockade, the Navy's overriding task must be to defeat the U-boats.
The rest of the nation's effort had to be devoted to sustaining the Army
which had suffered such appalling casualties. In conjunction with the
French, this had to hold back the Germans now being reinforced
from their Eastern Front, following the Russians' collapse, until the
full weight of the Americans could be put into the line in 1919. A fleet
action was, nonetheless, still possible; the Scandinavian convoy
débâcles had obliged Beatty to include a division of dreadnoughts in
the covering force; Scheer might be tempted to attack one with the
whole High Seas Fleet. Whilst Beatty welcomed such a chance to
avenge the ships he had lost at Jutland, he feared that it might occur
when the Germans had just introduced a new edition of their naval
cipher and before Room 40 had succeeded in breaking it, so that the
Admiralty would be unable to give him sufficient warning to bring the
Grand Fleet to the scene before four of his battleships were over-
whelmed. This nearly happened in April 1918. Profiting at last from
experience, Scheer concealed his intentions by forbidding the in-
discriminate use of wireless. Fortunately for the convoy his intelligence
was faulty; it had entered the Forth by the time the High Seas Fleet
reached the Norwegian coast; and while Hipper's battlecruisers were
making a vain search towards Bergen, the *Moltke* lost a propeller and
suffered a flooded engine-room. Her captain's signal reporting this
disabling accident was intercepted by the Admiralty who ordered the
Grand Fleet out from Rosyth, to which it had recently moved from
Scapa. But, realizing that the *Moltke*'s signals had deprived him of the
surprise on which he counted, Scheer had lost no time in ordering
his fleet to retire towards Heligoland, after detaching the *Oldenburg* to
take the damaged battlecruiser in tow. By nightfall he was south of
Beatty's line of advance so that he regained the safety of the Jade
without further incident, except for a torpedo hit on the hapless
Moltke from a British submarine.

The summer of 1918 brought a startling change in the fortunes of the
Allies. Germany was dismayed by Keyes' spirited attacks on Zeebrugge
and Ostend in April, even though they failed to block these U-boat
havens for long. Ludendorff's spring offensive, the *Kaiserschlacht* in
Champagne, was nearly successful in reaching Paris, but a million
fresh U.S. troops helped the Allies to effect a crushing *riposte* on the

Marne. On 8th August, 'the black day of the German Army' (*Ludendorff's own phrase*), Haig, whose men had so recently been fighting with their 'backs to the wall', advanced nine miles. By September Ludendorff's troops were retreating all along the Western Front. Above all, and sooner than had been hoped, the Grand Fleet's blockade sapped Germany's will for war. For more than a year the *Reichstag* had been under pressure from Erzeberger's Social Democrats to negotiate peace. Now it faced not only the prospect of military defeat but an incipient revolution incited by popular discontent with the growing shortages, especially of food, which the people had to suffer. On 5th October a new Chancellor, Prince Max of Baden, appealed to President Wilson for an armistice. With this move came indications that Scheer, who had become Chief of Naval Staff in July, would order the High Seas Fleet out for a final sortie; even a partial victory would be a useful card at the conference table. Hipper, now Commander-in-Chief, planned an attack on shipping in the Thames, covered by his Battle Fleet, which he hoped would draw the Grand Fleet south so that they could be brought to action off Terschelling; but what success this 'death ride' would have had, and whether the Grand Fleet could have reached the scene and with what result, was never put to the test. The High Seas Fleet, which had already suffered a serious mutiny in July and August 1917, had been inactive too long; its morale was not proof against the forces of discontent that were gaining ascendancy in Germany; when Hipper gave the order to sail on 29th October, his ships hoisted the Red Flag. The Kaiser's one hope of victory at sea, the U-boat campaign, had been abandoned already.

Although Jellicoe had completely reorganized the Naval Staff to achieve greater efficiency at the Admiralty, and had accepted the need to introduce the convoy system, he was not allowed to garner the fruits of these changes. His pessimism lost him Lloyd George's confidence; he lacked a sympathetic Press such as Beatty enjoyed; and he could not accept the autocratic methods of his First Lord, Sir Eric Geddes.* At the end of 1917 he was summarily dismissed and replaced by the ductile Wemyss, who thus became Britain's naval armistice negotiator. At Beatty's insistence Wemyss pressed for the

---

* He was not alone in objecting to Geddes' methods. Beatty took strong exception to them, notably when the First Lord usurped his authority by dictating the composition of the Grand Fleet's Court of Inquiry into the two German attacks on the Scandinavian convoys.

surrender of Germany's Fleet. This was opposed not only by the German delegates but by the U.S. Admiral Benson. Foch, whom the Allies had belatedly accepted as Supreme Army Commander, whose chief concern was to end the slaughter on land, imposed a compromise: the U-boats should be surrendered; the High Seas Fleet would be interned until its future might be settled by a peace conference. On 11th November King George V wrote in his diary: 'The great day has come and we have won the war'. Nine days after the Armistice the greater part of the High Seas Fleet made its last sortie; on the morning of 21st November 1918, it met the Grand Fleet without firing a shot, a triumph without previous parallel in British history which was only spoiled by Beatty's failure to invite Fisher or Jellicoe to share it as his guests onboard the *Queen Elizabeth*. 'The German ensign is to be hauled down at sunset,' signalled Beatty after the High Seas Fleet had anchored in the Forth, 'and is not to be hoisted again without permission.'*

If the prestige of the British Navy had been tarnished by its failure to achieve a major victory at Jutland, it was now at its peak. The decisive consequences of the battle were clear. By his failure to break the Grand Fleet's blockade Scheer had been driven to revive the unrestricted U-boat campaign, and this had not only been defeated but had impelled America into the war. And the combined effects of the blockade on the German people and, to a lesser extent, the arrival of U.S. troops in France, had enabled the Allied armies to humble Germany's military might. The High Seas Fleet died with the signing of the Peace Treaty in June 1919; taking advantage of armistice terms which allowed their crews to remain onboard without hindrance from British guards, the Germans scuttled their ships ingloriously below the placid waters of Scapa Flow. Hitler never revived its bombastic title, since nothing could have been more complete than its failure to achieve the ambition of the arrogant Wilhelm II, now an abdicated monarch exiled in neutral Holland, and his disciple, Grand Admiral von Tirpitz, to break Britain's command of the sea.

Jutland was, therefore, decisive in enabling the Allies to win the war—but a study of the battle cannot be left there. Two questions must be answered: why Jutland was not a clear victory for either side, and whether Jellicoe or Scheer could have made it so. For the German

* The U-boats surrendered to Tyrwhitt's Harwich Force.

Commander-in-Chief the answer to the first question is quickly given: he was under orders to avoid action with more than an inferior part of the Grand Fleet. As for the second, Germany was a Continental Power whose chief weapon was a magnificent army which would have gained a victory in France if it had not been rashly committed to a war on two fronts. Failure to realize that Britain's maritime power rested on her Mercantile Marine as well as on the Royal Navy, had led Tirpitz to make the fundamental error of designing a surface fleet whose ships could not, for lack of the necessary endurance, break out of the North Sea and operate against trade—a lesson which the Navy of the Third Reich was quick to learn. The chances that a naval action in 1916 or later would have done enough damage to the Grand Fleet to break the blockade were too small to justify the risk of losses in the High Seas Fleet which Germany could not replace. When U-boats had shown that they could do so much damage to Britain's jugular vein, the High Seas Fleet was best kept 'in being' to prevent a close blockade of their U-boat bases, to occupy British destroyers which would otherwise have been used to combat them, and to ensure that the Allies could not use their main element of naval power for operations, such as an amphibious landing on the German north-west coast, which would have directly endangered the Homeland.

Of Jellicoe the same two questions require more detailed consideration. The mistakes and signalling errors by the British ships, most of which had been made at the Dogger Bank and in other operations of the past two years of war—and could, if not should, have been learned from them; the failure of their admirals and captains to make enemy reports; the lack of co-operation between Room 40OB and the Admiralty War Room; the deficiencies in British gunnery and in ship and shell design—none of these is sufficient to explain why the Grand Fleet, with its considerable superiority and the *mystique* of the Royal Navy's near-invincible reputation, failed to win on 31st May. 'He who has made no mistakes in war has never made war' (*Turenne*). There were more fundamental reasons which contain lessons for all time for those whose business is war at sea.

> In the afternoon [of 1st June] Beatty came into the *Lion*'s chart-house. Tired and depressed, he sat down on the settee and closed his eyes. Unable to hide his disappointment at the result of the battle, he repeated in a weary voice, 'There is something wrong with our ships', then opening his eyes he added, '*and something wrong with our system*'.* (*Chalmers*)

* Author's italics.

The development of the 'great gun', with its broadside mounting, suggested the line-ahead duel as the better alternative to the *mêlée* which characterized naval actions before the Armada. It was used successfully by Blake, Deane and Monk against the Dutch at the Gabbard and Scheveningen (1653). The *Fighting Instructions* of 1691 added the principle of centralized control; they not only specified the line-ahead duel but forbade any departure from it 'till the main body be disabled or run'; though the battle fleet was divided into van, centre and rear squadrons, it was to be rigidly controlled by the admiral in the centre. ('The Captain General should be stationed in the centre squadron so that he may see those which go before and those which follow', wrote Alonzo de Chavez in 1530.) Barfleur (1692) and Malaga (1703), at which Rooke threatened dire penalties for any captain who quit the line without orders, seemed to confirm the wisdom of these instructions. In the eighteenth century many admirals believed the line-ahead duel to be the only method of fighting a naval action; thus Graves lost the opportunity to destroy De Grasse's fleet at the Chesapeake (1781). There were, however, some who departed from it by engaging only a part of the enemy's line and paid the price of failure, notably Mathews at Toulon (1744) and Byng at Minorca (1756). There was a third school who realized the limitations of the *Permanent Fighting Instructions* against a French fleet reluctant to stand and fight, and who therefore evolved their own variations; thus Rodney broke the enemy's line so successfully at the Saintes (1782) that none dared criticize him. Last, but most important, were those bold enough to disregard the *Instructions*; Anson at the First Battle of Finisterre (1747), Hawke at Quiberon Bay (1750) and Byron at Grenada (1779) ordered a general chase as soon as they realized that a line-ahead gun-duel was impossible with a French fleet intent on avoiding action. The dead hand of the *Permanent Fighting Instructions* was lifted by their success, together with Boscawen's at Lagos (1759) and Rodney's at the Moonlight Battle (1780). Their successors had the further advantage of the signal codes developed by Howe, Kempenfelt and Popham. With their aid Howe broke the enemy's line at many points at the Glorious First of June (1794); at St Vincent (1797) Nelson quit the line to forestall a likely enemy escape and Jervis, appreciating his action, ordered other ships to his support; at Camperdown (1797) Duncan approached in two lines and divided the Dutch into three; at Trafalgar Collingwood's division attacked Villeneuve's rear whilst Nelson's broke through his centre and threw the Combined Fleets into confusion.

From these centuries of experience two lessons emerged: the centrally controlled, line-ahead gun-duel was seldom decisive, and 'fighting instructions' must not be regarded as inflexible orders. Nonetheless, once Napoleon was out of the way, rigidity was reimposed in a new set of *Instructions* issued in 1816. As with the convoy system, a priceless piece of experience was relegated to the limbo of the supposed irrelevant past. The line-ahead gun-duel was re-established as the basis of naval tactics because 'it obviates the unpleasant necessity for serious and sustained thinking in advance and for rapid alterations in an emergency; and by placing no responsibility on subordinates, prevents giving them an opportunity to make mistakes' (*Richmond*). The only accepted solution out of the likely *impasse*, proved by Tsushima but difficult to achieve, was one way of concentrating on a part of the enemy's line, 'crossing the T'. Nonetheless, a few admirals advocated another solution, 'divided tactics'; Admiral Sir William May, whilst commanding the Home Fleet in 1910–11, carried out many exercises in which divisional commanders were given a relatively free hand to manœuvre their ships so as to concentrate a superior force on part of the enemy's line. In his own words: 'Dividing the fleet gives freedom to subordinates and in so doing strikes at the root of the purely defensive formation of the single line and leads to an offensive method of engaging the enemy.' The co-ordination of such attacks was, however, difficult and his successor abandoned them; and though Callaghan revived them, and Jellicoe accepted them, albeit in a modified form, especially for use by his fast Fifth Battle Squadron, he did little in the numerous exercises which he conducted in the two years prior to Jutland to practise his ships in anything but the rigid line. Jellicoe's clinical mind dwelt too much on centralized command; he issued battle *orders*, not *instructions*, and the concept of strict obedience inbred in his subordinates—'Every officer is to follow the motions of the Senior Officer present in regard to the performance of any evolution or the carrying out of any duty' (*King's Regulations and Admiralty Instructions*)—resulted in these 75 pages being accepted as dogma by all except the more spirited young destroyer captains. He discouraged those who pressed for changes, notably Sturdee who was a strong believer in 'divided tactics' and who said after Jutland: 'Had I had the starboard wing position I should have disobeyed the deployment signal and led my squadron to the other side of the Germans. If you wish to destroy your enemy you must put a net round him.' Lacking the 'Nelson touch', Jellicoe expected his captains always to conform with written orders; he did not realize that with so large a fleet, much of it beyond his sight, success would depend on personal explanations of his intentions, and upon his admirals' and captains' initiative in executing them in the light of the prevailing circumstances.

Two of these were particularly important at Jutland: the visibility and the few hours of daylight remaining after the Battle Fleets made contact. 'Was it likely that the weak and less heavily gunned German Fleet would expose itself to destruction in order to conform to our conception of how a battle should be fought?' (*Dewar*).

> With the Grand Fleet now in sight [wrote Captain Cowan of the *Princess Royal*] and within striking distance we felt like throwing our caps in the air—it looked a certainty that we had them. The Germans were confronted by our preponderant Battle Fleet, itching for blood after two years of waiting. Then, however, began that desperate, pompous business of the Grand Fleet's deployment. It had ever been beyond my intellect to grasp the value of it. What *we* were longing for was for just *one* of their divisions of eight to tag in astern of us and give that extra bit of punch which could crumple the head of their line.

Twenty-seven dreadnoughts (*i.e.* less the *Warspite*) might have achieved a very different result against 16, plus six older ships, if Jellicoe's Second and Fourth Battle Squadrons had deployed to the east of the German Battle Fleet, and the First and Fifth to the west. Scheer's *Kehrtwendung* would have availed him little; caught between the fires of two forces not significantly inferior to his own, he must have accepted battle or attempted flight to the south, leaving Mauve's slow squadron to its fate; with Tyrwhitt and Bradford's ships ahead, he would have had small hope that more than a tithe of his fleet would regain its harbours by one of the southern routes. It is, however, far easier to suggest this now than it could have been for Jellicoe to order it, or for Burney to do it on his own initiative, on 31st May 1916. 'None of my critics,' wrote Jellicoe, 'appear to have realized the extent to which the absence of information regarding the High Seas Fleet and the lack of visibility affected my handling of the

Fleet.'* Neither he nor Beatty is to be denigrated because he lacked the qualities of genius.

The second major reason for Jutland's result was Jellicoe's caution, frankly expressed in his letter to the Admiralty in October 1914 (see p. 39), and exemplified by his alterations away from enemy torpedo fire and his slow reaction to Scheer's two 'battle turns'. 'The lessons of the fight, written into my soul, were that if you do not seize your chances when they offer you will never get them again. Also, that when the chance is offered for a superior fleet to strike, it might be better to forget all about torpedoes. The damage from German torpedo attack that day was trifling compared with what their gunfire achieved' (*Cowan*). In 1916 Jellicoe placed too much emphasis on the hazards of U-boat attack during a fleet action; he had an unwarranted belief that the enemy would sow minefields in its wake; and he attached an importance to enemy torpedo fire which it never merited (in marked contrast to the small importance which he attached to the use of this weapon by his own ships). His caution stemmed from four factors.† One was inherent in his intellectual approach to every problem. The second was the British Navy's excessive preoccupation with the technical inventions which flowered in the decade preceding 1914, and the importance attached to material strength embodied in the dreadnought race with Germany, coupled with the parallel neglect of the human element, especially the need to develop 'captains of war' as well as 'captains of ships'. 'The artist is greater than his materials, the warrior than his arms; and it was in the man rather than in his weapons that the [British] Navy of the eighteenth century wrought its final triumph' (*Mahan*). The third factor was one with which no previous British admiral had had to contend since the Armada; when Rodney, Howe, Jervis and Nelson gained their victories, they hazarded only a third of Britain's battle fleet. The Kaiser's strategy compelled

---

* In *The World Crisis* Churchill wrote: 'He had only to tell the four "Queen Elizabeths" to attack separately the disengaged side of the enemy. What could be easier than for them to swoop round upon the old "Deutschland" squadron and cripple or destroy two or three of those in a few minutes?' Apart from the fact that by the relevant time the four 'Queen Elizabeths' had been reduced to an effective three, Jellicoe did not know until later that Scheer had brought Mauve's ships to sea.

† A fifth is sometimes added. Both the *Grand Fleet Battle Orders* and Beatty's own instructions contained references to the best fighting ranges for their ships, taking into account the thicknesses of armour in the two fleets among other factors. Jellicoe, in particular, was well aware that the German battleships and battle-cruisers were better protected than his own.

the Admiralty to entrust the whole of it to one man. Had Villeneuve destroyed Nelson's 27 ships-of-the-line, 54 would have been left to keep Britain's moat; Jellicoe could not risk all but a small handful of his country's dreadnoughts 'to gain or lose it all'.

Jellicoe's fourth justification was even more fundamental.

> It is absolutely necessary to look at the war as a whole, and to avoid being parochial, keeping our eyes on the German Fleet only. What we have to do is to starve and cripple *Germany*, to destroy *Germany*. The destruction of the German Fleet is a means to an end and not an end in itself. If in endeavouring to destroy the German Fleet we run risks which may prejudice our success in the greater object of destruction of Germany, those risks are too great. (*Richmond*)

Successive Cabinets, with no experience and little knowledge of war, had allowed the War Office to commit its relatively small military strength to the Continent, thereby making the defence of France the cornerstone of British strategy. (The belief that Britain would necessarily face defeat if the Channel ports fell was exposed as fallacious in 1940.) Britain's fleet, the most powerful in the world, was relegated to a secondary role; too few soldiers were then left to be used for the army's proper purpose, amphibious operations against the enemy's flanks. The Nation and the Empire were lured into pouring a generation of young men into Flanders, and into employing more of their resources than they could afford in sustaining them. The Fleet was only required to ensure that neither was interrupted, and to deny help to Germany's war potential from overseas. This role was essentially a defensive one; the Grand Fleet was not to be hazarded for the sake of destroying an enemy fleet whose influence on events in France was marginal, especially when it might be required to protect trade against another fleet deployed in the Atlantic if the United States should be provoked by the British blockade into siding with Germany. 'The British have only the stupidity of the Germans to thank for saving them from having a very serious situation develop in their relations with this country in the spring of 1916' (*Robert Lansing, U.S. Secretary of State*). After the first weeks of the war had committed the Allied armies to years of stalemate in France, no one could say that the Grand Fleet ought to be hazarded in order to destroy the High Seas Fleet. 'Most experienced commanders would probably have acted as Jellicoe did: his was a weapon on which the world depended. He was not prepared to take immeasurable risks' (*Chatfield*). 'He fought to make a German victory impossible rather than a British victory certain' (*Falls*). But 'a perception that a decisive battle is not a necessity in a particular situation, and ought not to be purchased at a heavy risk, should not engender a defensive habit of mind or scheme of tactics'. (*Churchill*)

Beatty did more than recognize the first of these reasons for the limited results of Jutland; whilst Jellicoe made a number of amendments to his *Battle Orders* which the action had shown to be needed, and introduced night gunnery practices, his successor as Commander-in-Chief undertook a complete revision, issued in the middle of 1917, which was a

> marked advance in tactical thought. The extremely mathematical principles culminating in a battle plan on an established form, disappear and in their place we have a clear, short exposition of principles marked by a high degree of courage and preparedness to accept risks. If such orders had been in existence on 31st May last year, and officers had thoroughly imbibed the spirit of them and acted upon them, I make small doubt that the High Seas Fleet would have been destroyed. It is of course only just to add that those orders may be in part the outcome of experience of that battle. (*Richmond*)

Unfortunately Beatty was not given the chance to prove these instructions, nor to show that, though he was obliged to accept a defensive strategy, this did not extend to his tactics. It may be said that Jellicoe lacked fire in his belly but, to be fair, it is possible that Beatty had it to excess; that he might have been as reckless with his handling of the whole Grand Fleet as he was with the Battlecruiser Fleet during the initial stages of Jutland. To conclude with the wise words of a German writer:

> There are those who maintain that the [British] naval policy of caution was a mistaken one. They claim that failure to use the Allied Fleets aggressively on opportune occasions resulted in needless prolongation of the war; that the submarine campaign, and the enormous losses in doubtful land battles, have proved that the policy of conservation involved greater risk than would have been incurred by the employment of aggressive strategy and tactics to gain decisive victories at sea. What sea power actually accomplished should be appreciated. At the same time, it should also be appreciated that the navies did not use their opportunities to accomplish more. *The seat of the trouble was not in the individuals but in the system which had rested satisfied with material preparation alone and had left neglected or incomplete the study of plans for actual war and the development of skill in the conduct of naval campaigns.**

* Author's italics.

But a dogmatic system of tactics which could not achieve a decisive result, allied to a too rigid concept of obedience to orders, was only one chain which bound both Jellicoe and Beatty. There was also a mis-conceived strategy which neglected Britain's principal weapon, which failed to use the superior strength of the Royal Navy to turn the flanks of Germany's military power. Neither chain was of their own making and, in the Grand Fleet, neither Admiral had the 'admixture of madness'—Aristotle's definition of genius—to break the one, nor the power to influence the other before it was too late.

For Scheer and Hipper Jutland spelled the end of the first fleet to throw down the gauntlet to British sea power for more than 100 years. Their naval careers ended, both men retired from public life, only Scheer's voice being heard through the pages of his two books about the war. His place in history assured, he died in 1928 just when he was looking forward to visiting England as Jellicoe's guest. Hipper out-lived him by four years; the German Navy has produced no greater commander even though he lacked the personal qualities needed to rouse his men for the High Seas Fleet's last desperate gamble in October 1918. Its architect, Tirpitz, was in the *Reichstag* from 1924 to 1928 when he was chiefly responsible for persuading Hindenburg to accept nomination for the presidency, and several contentious books came from his pen before he died in 1930. All three thus passed into the wings before the modest fleet which the Treaty of Versailles allowed Germany to keep was rebuilt to make a second attempt to challenge Britain's maritime power.

Of the British trio, Fisher died in 1920, mourned by many as the greatest admiral since Nelson. Immediately after the war Jellicoe made a world tour to advise the Dominions on their navies before serving as Governor-General of New Zealand. In subsequent retire-ment, until his death in 1935, his chief interest was the British Legion and the welfare of those who had fought under him. Beatty remained in command of the Grand Fleet until it was dispersed in March 1919. From November of that year until 1927 he was First Sea Lord, fighting the hardest battle of his life, to maintain the strength of the British Navy against the apathy of a war-weary, impoverished nation. He lived long enough to be able to insist, though suffering from influenza, on walking behind Jellicoe's coffin. Four months later he, too, was buried by a grateful nation in the crypt of St Paul's. For none can justly deny these three, as creator and commanders of the greatest fleet of capital ships the world will ever see, chief credit for the ultimate defeat of Germany and the humiliating end of the High Seas Fleet at Scapa Flow. Moreover, their legacy was not what Fisher called 'the tragedy' of Jutland, but a navy freed of its chains, one which, though much reduced in strength by the Washington and London Treaties, showed all the old Nelsonic skill when it was again called upon to defend Britain's moat in 1939, with Pound of the *Colossus* at the helm. Harwood did not hesitate to match the *Exeter*, *Ajax* and *Achilles* against the more powerful *Graf Spee*. Tovey of the *Onslow*, now in command of the Home Fleet, brought the *Bismarck* to bay. Cunningham, with a Mediterranean Fleet which had been schooled by Chatfield of the *Lion* and W. W. Fisher of the *St Vincent* to fight a night action, showed the old aggressive spirit against a stronger enemy, destroying much of it at Taranto and Matapan. Fraser hunted and sank the *Scharnhorst*. Noble and Horton achieved victory against the U-boats in the Battle of the Atlantic. Above all, the British Navy and Mercantile Marine were used to transport large armies overseas whereby first in North Africa, next in Sicily and Italy, and finally across the Channel, Germany's second attempt to conquer Europe was decisively defeated.

Jellicoe paid this tribute in one of his Jutland Dispatches:

> Sir David Beatty showed his fine qualities of gallant leadership, firm determination and correct strategic insight. He appreciated the situation at once on sighting first the enemy's lighter forces, then his battlecruisers, and finally his battle fleet. I can fully sympathize with his feelings when the evening mist and failing light robbed the Fleet of that complete victory for which he had manœuvred and for which the vessels in company with him had striven so hard. The services rendered by him, not only on this, but on two previous occasions have been of the very greatest value.

Twenty years later Beatty wrote in *The Times*:

> Jellicoe epitomized all the highest ideals for which the British Navy stands. The country owes a deep debt of gratitude to him for the valiant work he did during the war. He was an upright man and a model of integrity in everything he undertook. The tradition of the British Navy meant a great deal to him, and it can be said that he was an Admiral who made that tradition even more glorious.

The Nation delivered its verdict in 1948 in the words of the Duke of Gloucester when he unveiled bronze busts of both Admirals:

Together [they] led the Royal Navy through the last crisis of the long centuries when sea power depended upon ships and seamen alone. Their names bridge the gulf between the classic tradition of Trafalgar and the onset of total war as it is known today. They were buried in St Paul's Cathedral twelve years ago; but it is right that we should do them this final honour in Trafalgar Square, beside the monument of our greatest seaman and on the anniversary of his greatest victory.

Jellicoe and Beatty may not merit columns as high as Nelson's, but they well earned niches where, in the words of Admiral Hopwood,

> *On such the cryptic sightless eye is cast*
> *Of one with neither words nor time to spare,*
> *Only too thankful both have joined at last*
> *His lonely vigil in Trafalgar Square.*

APPENDIX I

The British Grand Fleet at Jutland

THE BATTLE FLEET

Battleships

(in order from van to rear when deployed)

SECOND BATTLE SQUADRON

King George V	Captain F. L. Field*
	(Flagship of Vice-Admiral Sir Martyn Jerram)
Ajax	Captain G. H. Baird
Centurion	Captain M. Culme-Seymour
Erin	Captain The Hon. V. A. Stanley
Orion	Captain O. Backhouse
	(Flagship of Rear-Admiral A. C. Leveson)
Monarch	Captain G. H. Borrett
Conqueror	Captain H. H. D. Tothill
Thunderer	Captain J. A. Fergusson

FOURTH BATTLE SQUADRON

Iron Duke	Captain F. C. Dreyer
	(Fleet flagship of Admiral Sir John Jellicoe)†
Royal Oak	Captain C. Maclachan
Superb	Captain E. Hyde-Parker
	(Flagship of Rear-Admiral A. L. Duff)
Canada	Captain W. C. M. Nicholson
Benbow	Captain H. W. Parker
	(Flagship of Vice-Admiral Sir Doveton Sturdee)
Bellerophon	Captain E. F. Bruen
Téméraire	Captain E. V. Underhill
Vanguard	Captain J. D. Dick

FIRST BATTLE SQUADRON

Marlborough	Captain G. P. Ross
	(Flagship of Vice-Admiral Sir Cecil Burney)

* Later Admiral of the Fleet Sir Frederick Field, First Sea Lord 1930–32.

† Jellicoe's staff included his brother-in-law, Vice-Admiral Sir Charles Madden, as Chief of Staff, who later became an Admiral of the Fleet and succeeded Beatty as First Sea Lord in 1926; and Commander, later Admiral of the Fleet Sir Charles Forbes, who was Commander-in-Chief Home Fleet at the outset of the Second World War.

Revenge	Captain E. B. Kiddle
Hercules	Captain L. Clinton-Baker
Agincourt	Captain H. M. Doughty
Colossus	Captain A. D. P. R. Pound*
	(*Flagship of* Rear-Admiral E. F. A. Gaunt)
Collingwood	Captain J. C. Ley
Neptune	Captain V. H. G. Bernard
St Vincent	Captain W. W. Fisher†

Note 1 Of these ships nine were armed with ten 12-inch guns, and one with fourteen, eleven with ten 13·5-inch guns, one with ten 14-inch, and two with eight 15-inch. Their turrets were centreline mounted so that the whole armament could be fired on either broadside, except for six of the 12-inch gunned ships in which two turrets were mounted so that their broadsides were limited to eight guns. All had a secondary armament of sixteen–twenty 4-inch or twelve–twenty 6-inch guns and were equipped with two-four 18-inch or 21-inch submerged torpedo tubes. With armour belts 9–13 inches and turret armour 8–13 inches thick, their displacements ranged from 18,600 to 28,000 tons, whilst their maximum speed was 21–22 knots.

Battlecruisers

(temporarily attached)

THIRD BATTLECRUISER SQUADRON

Invincible	Captain A. L. Cay
	(*Flagship of* Rear-Admiral The Hon. H. L. A. Hood)
Inflexible	Captain E. H. F. Heaton-Ellis
Indomitable	Captain F. W. Kennedy

Note 2 These ships were armed with eight 12-inch guns (two turrets in echelon limited their broadsides to six guns), sixteen 4-inch guns and five 18-inch submerged torpedo tubes. With a 6-inch armour belt and 7-inch turrets, they displaced 17,250 tons and had a maximum speed of 25 knots.

Armoured Cruisers

FIRST CRUISER SQUADRON

Defence	Captain S. V. Ellis
	(*Flagship of* Rear-Admiral Sir Robert Arbuthnot)
Warrior	Captain V. B. Molteno
Duke of Edinburgh	Captain H. Blackett
Black Prince	Captain T. P. Bonham

* Later Admiral of the Fleet Sir Dudley Pound, who was First Sea Lord during the greater part of the Second World War.

† Later Admiral Sir William Fisher, who was a distinguished Commander-in-Chief Mediterranean in the early 1930s.

SECOND CRUISER SQUADRON

Minotaur	Captain A. C. S. H. D'Aeth
	(*Flagship* of Rear-Admiral H. L. Heath)
Hampshire	Captain H. J. Savill
Cochrane	Captain E. La T. Leatham
Shannon	Captain J. S. Dumaresq

Note 3 These cruisers had a mixed armament of four–six 9·2-inch (four 7·5-inch in the *Hampshire*) and ten 6-inch or 7·5-inch (four 7·5-inch in the *Warrior* and *Cochrane*); also three–five 18-inch torpedo tubes. With a 6-inch armour belt on a displacement of 10,850–14,600 tons, they had a maximum speed of 23 knots.

Light Cruisers

FOURTH LIGHT CRUISER SQUADRON

Calliope	Commodore C. E. Le Mesurier
Constance	Captain C. S. Townsend
Caroline	Captain H. R. Crooke
Royalist	Captain The Hon. H. Meade
Comus	Captain A. G. Hotham

ATTACHED*

Active	Captain P. Withers
Bellona	Captain A. B. S. Dutton
Blanche	Captain J. M. Casement
Boadicea	Captain L. C. S. Woollcombe
Canterbury	Captain P. M. R. Royds
Chester	Captain R. N. Lawson

Note 4 For guns these ships carried six–ten 4-inch, *or* ten 5·5 inch, *or* two–three 6-inch plus, plus six–eight 4-inch. They also mounted two–eight 21-inch torpedo tubes. Some had a 3–4-inch protective belt, others none, on displacements of 3,300–5,200 tons, with a maximum speed of 26–30 knots.

Destroyers

FOURTH FLOTILLA

Tipperary (Captain C. J. Wintour), *Acasta, Achates, Ambuscade, Ardent, Broke, Christopher, Contest, Fortune, Garland, Hardy, Midge, Ophelia, Owl, Porpoise, Shark, Sparrowhawk, Spitfire, Unity*

ELEVENTH FLOTILLA

Castor (light cruiser: Commodore J. R. P. Hawksley), *Kempenfelt, Magic, Mandate, Manners, Marne, Martial, Michael, Milbrook, Minion, Mons, Moon, Morning Star, Maunsey, Mystic, Ossory*

* Chiefly for repeating visual signals between units of the Battle Fleet.

TWELFTH FLOTILLA

Faulknor (Captain A. J. B. Stirling), *Maenad, Marksman, Marvel, Mary Rose, Menace, Mindful, Mischief, Munster, Narwhal, Nessus, Noble, Nonsuch, Obedient, Onslaught, Opal*

Note 5 With very few exceptions these destroyers were armed with two–three 4-inch guns and two–four 21-inch torpedo tubes on a displacement of 800–1,000 tons with a maximum speed of 30–35 knots. (For *Castor* see Note 4 above.)

Miscellaneous

Abdiel (Minelayer)
Oak   (Destroyer tender to fleet flagship)

THE BATTLECRUISER FLEET

Battlecruisers

(in order from van to rear)

| *Lion* | Captain A. E. M. Chatfield* |
| | (*Flagship of* Vice-Admiral Sir David Beatty) |

FIRST BATTLECRUISER SQUADRON

Princess Royal	Captain W. H. Cowan
	(*Flagship of* Rear-Admiral O. de B. Brock)
Queen Mary	Captain C. I. Prowse
Tiger	Captain H. B. Pelly

Note 6 Armed with eight 13·5-inch guns in centreline turrets and sixteen 4-inch (*Tiger* twelve 6-inch) and two (*Tiger* four) 21-inch submerged torpedo tubes, with 9-inch armour on both belt and turrets, these ships displaced 26,350 (*Tiger* 28,500) tons and had a maximum speed of 27 knots.

SECOND BATTLECRUISER SQUADRON

New Zealand	Captain J. F. E. Green
	(*Flagship of* Rear-Admiral W. C. Pakenham)
Indefatigable	Captain C. F. Sowerby

See Note 2 above

* Later Admiral of the Fleet Lord Chatfield, First Sea Lord 1932–35, Minister for Co-ordination of Defence at the outbreak of the Second World War.

Fast Battleships

(temporarily attached)

FIFTH BATTLE SQUADRON

Barham	Captain A. W. Craig
	(*Flagship of* Rear-Admiral H. Evan-Thomas)
Valiant	Captain M. Woollcombe
Warspite	Captain E. M. Phillpotts
Malaya	Captain The Hon. A. D. E. H. Boyle

Note 7 These ships were armed with eight 15-inch guns in centreline turrets, a secondary armament of fourteen 6-inch guns, and four 21-inch submerged torpedo tubes. With a 13-inch armour belt and 13-inch armour on their turrets, they displaced 27,500 tons, and had a maximum speed of 24 knots.

Light Cruisers

FIRST LIGHT CRUISER SQUADRON

Galatea	Commodore E. S. Alexander-Sinclair
Phaeton	Captain J. E. Cameron
Inconstant	Captain B. S. Thesiger
Cordelia	Captain T. P. H. Beamish (See Note 4 above)

SECOND LIGHT CRUISER SQUADRON

Southampton	Commodore W. E. Goodenough
Birmingham	Captain A. A. M. Duff
Nottingham	Captain C. B. Miller
Dublin	Captain A. C. Scott

THIRD LIGHT CRUISER SQUADRON

Falmouth	Captain J. D. Edwards
	(*Flagship of* Rear-Admiral T. D. W. Napier)
Yarmouth	Captain T. D. Pratt
Birkenhead	Captain E. Reeves
Gloucester	Captain W. F. Blunt

Note 8 The ships in both the above squadrons displaced 5,250–5,400 tons and had a 3-inch protective belt. Armed with eight 6-inch guns and two 21-inch torpedo tubes, they had a maximum speed of 25 knots.

Destroyers

FIRST FLOTILLA

Fearless (light cruiser: Captain C. D. Roper), *Acheron, Ariel, Attack, Badger, Defender, Goshawk, Hydra, Lapwing, Lizard*

NINTH AND TENTH FLOTILLAS (*combined*)

Lydiard (Commander M. L. Goldsmith), *Landrail, Laurel, Liberty, Moorsom, Morris, Termagent, Turbulent*

THIRTEENTH FLOTILLA

Champion (light cruiser: Captain J. U. Farie), *Moresby, Narborough, Nerissa, Nestor, Nicator, Nomad, Obdurate, Onslow, Pelican, Petard*

See Note 5 (except for *Fearless* and *Champion*, for which see Note 4)

Seaplane-Carrier

Engadine

The German High Seas Fleet at The Skagerrak

THE BATTLE FLEET

Battleships

(in order from van to rear)

THIRD BATTLE SQUADRON

König	Captain Brüninghaus
	(*Flagship* of Rear-Admiral Paul Behncke*)
Grosser Kurfürst	Captain E. Goette
Kronprinz Wilhelm	Captain C. Feldt
Markgraf	Captain Seiferling
Kaiser	Captain F. von Kayserlink
	(*Flagship* of Rear-Admiral Nordmann)
Kaiserin	Captain Sievers
Prinz Regent Luitpold	Captain K. Heuser

FIRST BATTLE SQUADRON

Friedrich der Grosse	Captain T. Fuchs
	(*Fleet flagship* of Vice-Admiral Reinhard Scheer)
Ostfriesland	Captain von Natzmer
	(*Flagship* of Vice-Admiral E. Schmidt)
Thüringen	Captain H. Küsel
Helgoland	Captain von Kameke
Oldenburg	Captain Höpfner
Posen	Captain Lange
	(*Flagship* of Rear-Admiral Engelhardt)
Rheinland	Captain Rohardt
Nassau	Captain H. Klappenbach
Westfalen	Captain Redlich

SECOND BATTLE SQUADRON

Deutschland	Captain H. Meurer
	(*Flagship* of Rear-Admiral Mauve)
Hessen	Captain R. Bartels

* Subsequently Chief of the German Naval Staff from 1920 to 1924, for the small fleet which the Treaty of Versailles allowed Germany to retain.

Pommern	Captain Bölken
Hannover	Captain W. Heine
	(*Flagship of* Rear-Admiral F. von Dalwigk zu Lichtenfels)
Schlesien	Captain F. Behncke
Schleswig-Holstein	Captain Barrentrapp

Note 1 The First and Third Squadrons comprised dreadnoughts of which four were armed with twelve 11-inch guns and four with twelve 12-inch, though all their broadsides were limited to eight. The others carried ten 12-inch guns. All had a secondary armament of fourteen 5·9-inch guns, and five–six 17·7 or 19·7-inch submerged torpedo tubes. With armour belts 11–14 inches thick and the same on their turrets, they displaced 18,900–25,390 tons and had a maximum speed of 22 knots. The Second Squadron comprised pre-dreadnoughts of 13,200 tons, armed with four 11-inch and fourteen 6·7-inch guns, plus six 17·7-inch submerged tubes. With 10-inch belts and 11-inch turret armour, their maximum speed was limited to 17 knots.

Light Cruisers

FOURTH SCOUTING GROUP

Stettin	Captain F. Regensburg
	(*Broad pendant of* Commodore von Reuter)
München	Commander O. Böcker
Hamburg	Commander von Gaudecker
Frauenlob	Captain G. Hoffmann
Stuttgart	Captain Hagedorn

Note 2 These ships of 2,700–3,500 tons, without a protective belt, were armed with ten 4·1-inch guns and two 17·7-inch torpedo tubes, and were capable of 21–23 knots.

Torpedoboats

| *Rostock* (light cruiser) | Captain O. Feldmann |
| | (*Broad pendant of* Commodore Michelson) |

FIRST FLOTILLA (half)
    4 boats under Commander C. Albrecht (in *G39*)

THIRD FLOTILLA
    7 boats under Captain Hollmann (in *S53*)

FIFTH FLOTILLA
    11 boats under Captain Heinecke (in *G11*)

SEVENTH FLOTILLA
    9 boats under Captain von Koch (in *S24*)

Note 3 German torpedoboats bore no name, only a single letter followed by a numeral. They varied in size from 800 tons, capable of a speed of 27 knots, to 1,800 tons with a speed of 37 knots, whilst their guns ranged from three 12-pounders to three 4-inch, and their torpedo tubes from three 17·7-inch to six 19·7-inch. (*Rostock*, which had a 2½-inch protective belt, displaced 4,900 tons, carried twelve 4·1-inch guns and four 19·7-inch torpedo tubes, and had a speed of 27 knots.)

THE BATTLECRUISER FORCE

Battlecruisers

FIRST SCOUTING GROUP

Lützow	Captain Harder
	(*Flagship of* Vice-Admiral Franz Hipper)*
Derfflinger	Captain Hartog
Seydlitz	Captain M. von Egidy
Moltke	Captain von Karpf
Von der Tann	Captain Hans Zenker†

Note 4 *Von der Tann* was armed with eight 11-inch guns, *Moltke* and *Seydlitz* with ten 11-inch, *Lützow* and *Derfflinger* with eight 12-inch. Their secondary armaments comprised ten to fourteen 5·9-inch guns, and they were equipped with four 17·7 or 19·7-inch submerged torpedo tubes. With a 10–12-inch armour belt and 9–11-inch armoured turrets, their displacements ranged from 21,000–28,000 tons, and they had maximum speeds between 25 and 30 knots.

Light Cruisers

SECOND SCOUTING GROUP

Frankfurt	Captain T. von Trotha
	(*Flagship of* Rear-Admiral Bödicker)
Wiesbaden	Captain Reiss
Pillau	Captain Mommsen
Elbing	Captain Madlung

Note 5 The first two of this group, with a 2½-inch protective belt, displaced 5,120 tons; the latter, with no belt, 4,350 tons. All were armed with eight 5·9-inch guns and two–four 19·7-inch torpedo tubes, and had a maximum speed of 28 knots.

* Hipper's senior staff officer was Commander Erich Raeder, future Grand Admiral of Hitler's Navy during the first part of the Second World War.
† Subsequently Chief of the German Naval Staff from 1924 to 1928.

APPENDIX II

Torpedoboats

Regensburg (light cruiser)   Captain Heuberer
                                       (*Broad pendant of* Commodore Heinrich)

SECOND FLOTILLA

    10 boats under Captain Schuur (in *B98*)

SIXTH FLOTILLA

    9 boats under Captain Schultz (in *G41*)

NINTH FLOTILLA

    11 boats under Captain Goehle (in *V28*)

See Note 3. (The *Regensburg* was similar to the *Rostock*.)

The Harper Record

'This, the first trial of strength between the two fleets, has been the most bitter disappointment of this terribly disappointing war. One's confidence, perhaps an overweening confidence in the power of the Fleet, is shaken.'

Lord Hankey on 2nd June 1916

Jutland came as such an anti-climax to a nation which had waited two years for its Navy to meet the Germans in a battle which was expected to be a triumph comparable with Trafalgar, that controversy was inevitable. There were, however, special reasons why the argument became so acute in Britain in the decade following the war, why it was sustained for so long, and why it still has a spark of life in it. The first was the communiqué hurriedly issued by the Admiralty, before Jellicoe could reach Scapa and telegraph his first report, in order to counteract the German claim to victory which Berlin trumpeted to the world after Scheer's earlier return to the Jade. The uninspired tone of this document may be judged from the quotations at the head of Chapters 3 and 5. It also contained such phrases as, 'among [the Battlecruiser Fleet] the losses were heavy', and catalogued them. Conversely, whilst it said that 'the enemy losses were serious', it could not be specific about them, nor emphasize the damage suffered by the surviving German ships. When the British Press and Public jumped to the conclusion that the Grand Fleet had been defeated, a reassuring account was composed, but since this could not transform the battle into the expected triumph, many suspected that the Admiralty was concealing the full truth.*

Within the Royal Navy debate was inevitable; the lessons of any battle should be analysed so that steps may be taken to rectify faults. But in this instance the Service was sharply divided between those who championed Jellicoe to the detriment of Beatty and *vice versa*; to the proper loyalties of those who served either in the Battle Fleet or in the Battlecruiser Fleet were added such factors as the older officers' resentment at Beatty's rapid promotion, and their dislike of his flamboyance which captured the imagination of

---

* *Cf.* the German handling of the news: '*1st June.* A telegram arrived re the battle. It is not clear whether we achieved any success. Our known losses make it appear very doubtful that we can call this a victory. *2nd June.* Several more telegrams arrived giving the estimated losses of the English which are 2:3 in our favour. The Kaiser was therefore able to announce, "We have won a great victory at sea".' (*Admiral von Müller*)

the younger officers.* The Press, which from the time of the Heligoland Bight action had built up Beatty's *panache* into an heroic image against which Jellicoe's quiet personality counted for little, tended to distort the engagement into a victory for the British battlecruisers, and ascribe Scheer's escape to Jellicoe's failure to handle his Battle Fleet with the same skill. (In particular a false interpretation, discreditable to Jellicoe, and never intended by Beatty, was placed on the latter's 1950 signal: 'Submit van of battleships follow battlecruisers. We can then cut off whole of enemy battle fleet'.) A disappointed Nation noted that, whilst Beatty superseded Jellicoe in command of the Grand Fleet and remained in this appointment until the High Seas Fleet had surrendered, Jellicoe was dismissed from the office of First Sea Lord at the end of 1917.

All this led Wemyss (who had not served in the Grand Fleet and was, therefore, without bias), on learning that Jellicoe intended to publish his own account of the battle,† to appoint a small committee under Captain J. E. T. Harper charged with compiling an official narrative of the battle, together with diagrams, on the basis of all available documentary evidence (*i.e.* the reports of flag officers and captains, ships' signal logs and track charts, etc.). Harper was thorough; for example, he arranged for the wreck of the *Invincible* to be located and fixed in order to reconcile the discrepancies between the navigational reckonings of the *Iron Duke* and the *Lion*; and he scrupulously avoided making comments, favourable or otherwise, on the conduct of the action. By way of ensuring that the result would be accepted as unprejudiced and so stifle ill-informed controversy, Wemyss decided that it should not be shown to either Jellicoe or Beatty before publication. Unfortunately, just after Harper had completed this *Record* in October 1919, Beatty succeeded Wemyss and thereby assumed, with the rest of the Board of Admiralty, responsibility for its publication. This allowed him to read the proofs, from which he realized that it did not show his conduct of the battle in the same favourable light as the Public had come to see it. Harper was therefore required to make a number of alterations to both text and plans. A Foreword was also added (not by Harper) which emphasized the part played by the battlecruisers and minimized that of the Battle Fleet.

Whilst Harper accepted most of Beatty's emendations, there were a few which he refuted with documentary evidence, maintaining that this was likely to be nearer the truth than any individual's recollection of events which had occurred more than three years before. Moreover, when he was overruled, he made a tactless demand for the inclusion of a note to the effect that he accepted no responsibility for the published version since it

---

* For such partisan feeling, which is never healthy in an Armed Service, the officers had been set a bad example by the fierce pre-war feud between Fisher and Beresford.

† *The Grand Fleet, 1914–1916*, which, like Scheer's *Germany's High Seas Fleet in the World War*, appeared in 1919–20. In the event neither work contributed much to the controversy since their authors necessarily dealt with the battle from their own limited view-points.

did not wholly accord with the documented facts. This dispute reached the ears of Jellicoe who, understandably, asked to see the *Record*. And his criticisms of some of Beatty's amendments, not to mention his much stronger objections to the Foreword, were only pacified by an assurance that the *Record* would be re-examined, nothing being published until he had agreed to it. But how to revise Harper's work to the satisfaction of both Jellicoe and Beatty placed the Board in such a dilemma that an objection by the prospective publishers of the *Official History*, that its sales would be prejudiced by the earlier appearance of the *Record*, was welcomed as sufficient reason for pigeon-holing it *sine die*.

This decision failed to allow for the fact that the First Lord had told Parliament that the *Record* was being prepared: caustic questions were asked, especially when Wemyss himself wrote to *The Times* in December 1920 regretting that the *Record* had not yet appeared. The publication of the *Jutland Dispatches* in the same month—'a vast mass of undigested facts from which the layman cannot possibly disentangle the true history of this great sea fight' (*The Globe*)—did nothing to allay public belief that the Admiralty had something to hide. The growing clamour for a reliable and readable record was, however, largely stilled by the appearance of the *Official History*, *Naval Operations, Volume III*, in 1923. Sir Julian Corbett did his work so well that his handicaps were not appreciated; he had no access to any detailed German account of Jutland, whilst for justifiable security reasons he was forbidden to disclose the signals deciphered by Room 40. On the other hand he was allowed to use the *Harper Record*. He also had access to the secret *Naval Staff Appreciation of Jutland* which had been prepared for distribution within the Navy. Unfortunately its joint authors, the brothers Captain K. G. B. and Commander A. C. Dewar, went beyond what was reasonable in their criticisms. No Board could be expected to accept a work which, whilst condemning so many aspects of the British conduct of the action, ignored many of the factors which made Jellicoe's and Beatty's tasks so difficult. Even from the dispassionate vantage of forty years later it seems surprising that it was allowed to reach the stage of cold print before the Admiralty ordered its destruction. Corbett's version, however, was not so easily disposed of; having died shortly after completing his manuscript he could not be asked to alter it, and the Board hesitated before 'doctoring' the work of an historian of repute. Their solution was the publication of a pedantically written *Narrative of the Battle of Jutland*; but this was quickly seen to be worse than biased in Beatty's favour. In partial fulfilment of the Admiralty's promise in connection with the disputed *Harper Record*, Jellicoe was allowed to read it before publication, and his numerous objections were met by the discourtesy of relegating them to an Appendix, to which were added many dissenting footnotes and the disclaimer, 'where the Appendix differs from the Narrative, Their Lordships are satisfied that the Narrative is more in accordance with the evidence available'. Fuel was added to the resulting fire by *Der Krieg zur See* (the German Official History) which, notwithstanding its attempt to prove the case for a German victory, threw fresh light on the handling of the British forces which was not always favourable to Beatty; by Churchill's misconceived comments on some aspects of the battle in *The World Crisis*; and by Admiral Sir Reginald Bacon's *The Jutland Scandal* (1925), whose sensational defence of Jellicoe was heightened by a threat of legal action by some of those who were too severely criticized for their partisan support of Beatty.

The controversy, in which Beatty was careful to ensure that he appeared to take no part, was still a live issue when he was superseded as First Sea Lord by Jellicoe's brother-in-law and Chief of Staff at Jutland. One of Admiral Sir Charles Madden's first actions was to authorize publication of Harper's *Record of the Battle of Jutland* in 1927 'to dispel the idea that there is any mystery, sensational evidence, or criticism contained in it', albeit without its diagrams because of the cost. In the same year Harper (by this time retired) issued *The Truth about Jutland*. These two works did much to cut the rival arguments down to size; at last, a decade after the war, it seemed possible to make an objective evaluation of the battle. The matter rested there until the late 'thirties, when Corbett's *Naval Operations, Volume III*, was revised; the new edition not only took into account the German Official History, but included the signals deciphered by Room 40 but not passed to Jellicoe, which made clear that Scheer was returning home by the Horn Reefs gap. When this appeared in 1940 the British Public was too concerned with another battle being fought in the skies over their heads for much to be written of the scant justice which Jellicoe had suffered from the Admiralty's inability to reveal before his death its significant contribution to Scheer's escape. It should, nonetheless, have put an end to controversy: as revised Corbett's work, together with *Der Krieg zur See*, reveal all the relevant facts about Jutland.

There are, however, some who still suppose that the whole truth has yet to be disclosed because it is known that, before his death, Harper entrusted certain documents appertaining to the battle to the Council of the Royal United Service Institution. Having been allowed access to these *Harper Papers*, the present author is able to dispel this illusion. They amount to a copy of the typescript of the *Record*, together with proofs of both the text and diagrams, on which are marked the alterations which Beatty required but which Harper contested, copies of the relevant Admiralty minutes, etc., covering the dispute, and Harper's subjective and somewhat embittered account of it. These show how Beatty tried to conceal his battlecruisers' poor gunnery, by 'manipulating' the *Record* covering the period 1700 to 1800 (the run north) to the disadvantage of the more efficient Fifth Battle Squadron; and how he attempted to magnify the small part played by his battlecruisers in repulsing Scheer's ill-judged attempt to force a way through the Grand Fleet after his initial 'battle turn' away, by likewise 'manipulating' the *Record* for the period 1800 to 1850. A specific example is the involuntary 360-degree turn by the *Lion* due to a compass failure (*vide* p. 114). (Notwithstanding much evidence to support this, and despite the fact that he was away from the bridge at the time examining the damage done to his flagship, Beatty insisted that he ordered a turn of 90 degrees to close the enemy which, through the compass failure, became an involuntary one of 180 degrees to starboard, and that this was corrected by a 180-degree turn to port. He does not seem to have realized that he was maintaining a fallacious position; if the initial turn had been intentional, the consequences of the compass failure should have been rectified by a turn to port of only 90 degrees.) The *Harper Papers* also contain Jellicoe's strong objections to the Foreword's implications that Beatty had successfully faced Hipper with an inferior force (*i.e.* the presence of the Fifth Battle Squadron was ignored), that Jellicoe was slow in bringing his Battle Fleet to Beatty's support and that, after coming within range of the High Seas Fleet, the British Battle Fleet took little part in the action. But this only reveals the details of an unhappy incident in the life of a great man; it does not throw fresh light on the battle itself. So the *Harper Papers* are of little real interest except to a future biographer of Beatty, or to a student of Admiralty administration during the years following the First World War.

In short, the Jutland controversy has been dead since 1940; since then it has been possible to tell the full story of the battle and to assess the merits of Jellicoe's and Beatty's handling of their fleets for their true worth. The reputations of these two leaders who were chiefly responsible for ensuring that the High Seas Fleet surrendered to the Grand Fleet in November 1918, cannot now be charred by raking over the dead embers of a once fierce argument that was kept ablaze for too long by a small human weakness in one of them. Beatty may have made use of his position as First Sea Lord to distort the truth about Jutland in his own favour, but lesser men have suffered *folie de grandeur* with smaller excuse. He had to carry more than the heavy burden of his Admiralty Office after the incessant strain of four-and-a-half years of war at sea; he bore without complaint the nagging worry of a neurotically sick wife to whom he remained patiently devoted. There are aspects of Nelson's life which are open to harsher criticism, but no one questions his right to look down on the heart of London from the summit of a column in Trafalgar Square.

SHORT BIBLIOGRAPHY

The following are among the more important, or for other reasons interesting, books dealing with Jutland, or the events which led up to and ensued from the battle, which have been published in English (*i.e.* including translations of German works):

ADMIRALTY British *Jutland Despatches*
    Narrative of the Battle of Jutland
    Record of the Battle of Jutland; prepared by Captain J. E. T. Harper
BACON, Admiral Sir R. H. *The Life of John Rushworth Earl Jellicoe*
CHALMERS, Rear-Admiral W. S. *The Life and Letters of David Beatty, Admiral of the Fleet*
CHATFIELD, Admiral of the Fleet Lord *The Navy and Defence*
CHURCHILL, Winston S. *The World Crisis, 1914–1918*
CORBETT, Julian, and NEWBOLT, Henry *History of the Great War based on Official Documents: Naval Operations*
DREYER, Admiral Sir Frederic *The Sea Heritage*
FAWCETT, H. W., and HOOPER, G. W. W. *The Fighting at Jutland*
FROST, Commander H., U.S. Navy *The Battle of Jutland*
GIBSON, Langhorne, and HARPER, Vice-Admiral J. E. T. *The Riddle of Jutland*
HARPER, Vice-Admiral J. E. T. *The Truth About Jutland*
HASE, Commander G. von, German Navy *Kiel and Jutland*
JAMESON, Rear-Admiral Sir William *The Fleet that Jack Built*
JELLICOE, Admiral Viscount John R. *The Grand Fleet, 1914–1916: Its Creation, Development and Work*
KEMP, Lieutenant-Commander P. K. *The Papers of Admiral Sir John Fisher* (Navy Records Society)
MACINTYRE, Captain Donald *Jutland*
MARDER, A. J. *Fear God and Dread Nought*
MARDER, A. J. *From the Dreadnought to Scapa Flow*
SCHEER, Admiral Reinhard, German Navy *Germany's High Seas Fleet in the World War*
TIRPITZ, Grand Admiral von, German Navy *My Memoirs*
WALDEMEYER-HARTZ, Hugo von *Admiral von Hipper*
WOODWARD, E. L. *Great Britain and the German Navy*

The most important work of which no English translation has been published, but of which a typescript English version is available in the British Admiralty Library, is the German official history, *Der Krieg zur See.*

Among unpublished sources which no serious student of the action can afford to neglect are the collections of papers and letters left by Admirals Jellicoe and Beatty and the Admiralty *Naval Staff Appreciation of Jutland* of which, fortunately for posterity, at least two copies eluded destruction (*vide* Appendix III).

Index

INDEX

The numerals in **heavy type** refer to the *figure numbers* of the illustrations. Ships are indexed under 'Warships', British and German, pp. 205–07.